THE BELLARMINE SERIES

Under the Direction of the Jesuit Fathers of
Heythrop College

General Editor
EDMUND F. SUTCLIFFE, S.J.
*Professor of Old Testament Exegesis and Hebrew
at Heythrop College*

A list of the Bellarmine Series
with Press appreciations wll be
found at the end of this volume ·

THE BELLARMINE SERIES X

SEX ENLIGHTENMENT AND THE CATHOLIC

BY

J. LEYCESTER KING, S.J.

*Professor of Psychology
at Heythrop College*

LONDON
BURNS OATES & WASHBOURNE LTD.
Publishers to the Holy See

1944

De Licentia Superiorum Ordinis:

FRANCISCUS MANGAN, S.J.

Praep. Prov. Angliae

Nihil Obstat :

FRIDERICUS C. COPLESTON, S.J.

Censor deputatus

Imprimatur :

✠ THOMAS

Archiepiscopus Birmingamiensis

Die 4a Maii 1944

TABLE OF CONTENTS

I
INTRODUCTION

Within recent years there has been considerable discussion regarding the sex enlightenment of the young, and there has been fairly general agreement that this important matter cannot be satisfactorily handled by the haphazard methods of the past. Systematic instruction of the young is now being undertaken to a gradually increasing extent, and certain organisations of national status offer the services of a panel of qualified lecturers, who are prepared not only to address Education Committees, Youth Committees, etc., but also to lecture on sex matters to audiences of schoolchildren and adolescents of various age ranges.

In general, those responsible for the education of Catholics have not availed themselves of these services, and indeed have tended to hold themselves very much aloof in the whole matter. Many non-Catholics have been frankly puzzled at this attitude and have drawn entirely wrong conclusions as to the motives dictating it. The writer has received so many enquiries on the subject, both from Catholics and non-Catholics, that in his opinion the time has come to write something to which he can refer his enquirers. This little book is only a tentative contribution and makes few, if any, pretensions. The writer has been impelled to undertake it by a sense of the urgency of the matter, rather than by any consciousness of his own competence. Consequently, rather than make any claims for the book, it seems suitable at the outset to set forth some of the things which it does *not* claim to be :—

(i) It is not intended as a complete philosophy of life.

(ii) For reasons which will become apparent later, it is not intended to furnish parents and teachers with an account of the actual facts which have to be communicated in the course of sex-enlightenment.

(iii) The book has no *official* status ; it is not put forward as an authoritative declaration of the Catholic attitude on this question. The writer has no authority to make such an authoritative declaration, though he believes that the opinions he expresses are in complete conformity with the various pronouncements on the subject which have from time to time been made by ecclesiastical authority.

(iv) There is no attempt at an exhaustive treatment of the whole topic of sex-enlightenment as such, since such an attempt is rendered impossible by the limited amount of time at the writer's disposal.

II
CATHOLIC TEACHING

At the end of this book are given a number of references to, and extracts from, authoritative ecclesiastical documents bearing on this subject : Papal allocutions, replies of Roman Congregations, etc. Let me right at the outset state quite unequivocally what is my own attitude to these documents. This question of the sex-enlightenment of the young is a very difficult one. There are, I know, those who take a different view and hold that it is all a very simple and matter-of-fact affair, easily grappled with, whether it be by means of co-education, or mixed bathing or nudism or nature-study in the schools, or a 'straight talk' from father, or by 'laissez faire and see what happens'. Neither as a priest nor as a psychologist can I agree with this view, and I have yet to be convinced that the techniques advocated are even remotely effective in producing adequate sex-adjustment. I believe that the sex-adjustment of the individual is a very delicate and 'nice' adjustment, and that to effect it satisfactorily a very wide and complex range of factors has to be taken into consideration. I shall show later that there are many questions to which I, and very many with me, can give no clear-cut and complete answers at the present. In this delicate field, human prudence walks in a very fumbling manner and it is only the superficial observer who thinks that the right road is easy to find. Now it is precisely in such cases that the authoritative guidance of the Holy See is most necessary and should be most welcomed. Such guidance, coming from the one authority on earth which is competent to make final pronouncements regarding man's nature, destiny and moral duties, is of immense value in facilitating a right approach to the subject. On grounds no higher than ordinary human prudence, it must be remembered that the Holy See does not make pronouncements on matters so important without the most careful consideration of all the issues involved. In these matters Rome issues her directions with a sense of responsibility unparalleled elsewhere in the world. I should regard it therefore as altogether unsound to seek a solution for these problems outside the framework laid down by the Holy See. As will appear more in detail later, that framework is abundantly wide enough for our task, and it is, moreover, quite unassailable from the point of view of scientific psychology.

At the same time, however, it must be remembered that these Roman pronouncements were, in most instances, addressed to the whole world, and could not therefore be expected to go into details in such a way as to meet the special requirements and circumstances of the widely differing cultures and conditions concerned. It follows, therefore, that a certain amount of careful work is called for, in applying the Holy See's more general instructions to the solution of particular problems presented by different localities, climates, and cultural, educational and social levels. It is as a small contribution towards such work that this little book has been written.

A SUMMARY OF THE HOLY SEE'S DIRECTIONS ON THIS MATTER

The Rescript of 18 January, 1908. In this document, addressed to the Bishop of Barcelona, the Sacred Congregation of the Index disapproved of the instruction and education of Spanish children in this matter being conducted along the lines laid down in the Spanish translations of two English books on sex-instruction current at the time. In view of the much clearer guidance given in subsequent documents we need not here discuss what conclusions, if any, can be drawn from this Rescript as far as English children in almost entirely different circumstances are concerned.

Rescript of 21 March, 1931. This was a reply from the Holy Office to the question: 'Can that method be approved which is known as "sexual education", or even "sexual initiation"'? Now if the Holy Office had simply replied 'No', we might have been left in some doubt as to the force of the answer, since it is not quite clear what precise form of sex-enlightenment or instruction is referred to in the question. It is known that in certain countries, about this time, methods of 'sexual initiation' or 'sexual instruction' for young children were being advocated and adopted which were gross, immoral and likely to have the worst effects on the children's moral attitude. Indeed, there is a certain amount of evidence that in some cases this was precisely the result aimed at. A condemnation by the Holy Office of such a diabolical procedure, though obviously entirely justified, would not afford much guidance for those who sought to impart the necessary information in a moral, constructive and Christian manner.

But the Holy Office was not content with a merely negative reply. It went further by laying down that the positive principles to be employed in the education of youths were those promulgated by Pius XI in his Encyclical on Christian Education of 31/12/29. The reply added a valuable summary of these principles, and ended by disapproving of certain unspecified current books which propagated novel methods of instruction, some of them written by Catholics.

The Encyclical ' Divini Illius Magistri ' of 31 December, 1929.— This is the famous Encyclical of Pius XI on the Christian Education of Youth, to which reference is made in the Rescript quoted above.

The Encyclical 'Casti Connubii' of 31 December, 1930.—This Encyclical is an authoritative declaration of the nature of Christian marriage. It is a very comprehensive document and its bearing on the subject of this book will be manifest.

The Papal Allocution of 21 October, 1941.—This pronouncement, addressed to mothers by Pius XII *viva voce*, is shorter than either of the Encyclicals referred to above. But in spite of its comparative brevity, it gives a masterly exposition of our subject, and deals with it in considerable detail. It forms a document of the highest value, and without it the writer would have shrunk from the task of producing this present book.

Let us now attempt to summarise for our own immediate purposes the points which emerge from these various documents, bearing in mind that such a summary must fall far short of the full message of the documents themselves.

(i) Further light on the nature of the 'sexual education' or 'sexual initiation' condemned in the Rescript of 21 March, 1931, may be gained by a study of certain passages in the other documents. Thus in his Encyclical *Divini Illius Magistri* Pius XI warns us against 'those who with dangerous assurance and under an ugly term propagate a so-called sex-education, falsely imagining they forearm youths against the dangers of sexuality by means purely natural, such as a foolhardy initiation and precautionary instruction for all indiscriminately, even in public; and, worse still, exposing them at an early age to the occasions, in order to accustom them, as it is argued, and, as it were, to harden them against such dangers.'

The same Pope, in his Encyclical *Casti Connubii*, had already stigmatised 'that exaggerated physiological education—laying much stress on these physiological matters, in which is learned rather the art of sinning in a subtle way than the virtue of living chastely.'

Thus we may conclude:

(*a*) Youth cannot be 'forearmed against the dangers of sexuality' by purely natural means. (This is a point of outstanding importance, and must clearly involve a somewhat sharp contrast between the Catholic approach to the matter, and the methods advocated by various public bodies and national voluntary organisations.)

(*b*) The use of the words 'foolhardy initiation' draws attention to the fact that a good deal of *prudence* is called for in this matter.

(*c*) Disapproval is expressed of instruction given to 'all indiscriminately even in public.' This suggests that it is the part of prudence to take into consideration such things as sex, age, social and cultural background, etc., in assessing the requirements of the young people to be instructed. Such considerations are obviously difficult to provide for where public instruction is resorted to. It does not, however, seem fair to conclude from this passage that all collective instruction, however prudently and reticently conducted, to carefully selected audiences of whatever age is positively forbidden. Though we do not consider that any form of collective instruction can meet requirements fully, we shall, later in this book, suggest various ways in which certain forms of collective instruction may prove useful, and in certain cases even indispensable. In doing so we do not feel that we are in conflict either with the letter or the spirit of this portion of the Holy See's directions.

(*d*) A hardening process carried out by exposing young people to stimulation of the sex urge is condemned. Such condemnation scarcely needs either explanation or defence. And yet this condemnation is not an idle one, since, even in this country, the 'hard-boiled' school of sex instructors fall under it to a large extent, especially those who do not hesitate in the face of the danger of releasing waves of emotion with quite unpredictable results among co-educational audiences.

(*e*) A warning is issued against instruction that is 'exaggeratedly physiological.'

Evidently the physiological side of things cannot be neglected in any instruction which can be regarded as adequate. Indeed, vagueness or inaccuracy in this matter can have results the reverse of those intended, with very serious repercussions in later adult life. But experienced lecturers on this subject know that unambiguous clearness and accuracy are quite compatible with due reticence and care to avoid unnecessary stimulation of the imagination. Within limits, the amount of physiological knowledge required is a function of the age of the individual under instruction, and the aim should be to give clearly, concisely and objectively just that amount of knowledge which is necessary or suitable at the particular time concerned. In this matter, the instructor should have a light, sensitive touch, and guard against 'projecting' on to his pupil the more aloof attitude engendered by his own more complete knowledge. In any case, the relevant physiological facts are simple and few, they can be transmitted without any embarrassment, and should be given with clearness and precision, yet with an economy which allays curiosity rather than with a detailed profusion which stimulates it.

(ii) Attention is drawn to the mistake which is constantly being made, of losing sight of the fact of Original Sin and the consequent essential weakness of human nature.

(iii) It thus comes about that mere information supplied to

the intellect is regarded as an adequate treatment of the problem by those who forget that the human will does not always follow the dictates of reason, and, consequently, stands in need of its own special training.

(iv) Paramount emphasis is laid on the necessity for the complete, stable and continuous instruction of youth of both sexes in religion. This is, of course, a point on which Catholic educators have always been insistent, and we are still severely penalised for that insistence, in spite of the fact that there is now general public recognition that the deterioration both in morality and in morale, and the alarming increase in delinquency, are closely connected with the appalling ignorance on religious matters obtaining in the population generally.

(v) Stress is laid on the *positive* side of the matter, by urging the inculcation of a high regard for purity, together with a desire and love for it. This stands in sharp contrast to the attitude of some of our sex-educators in this country, to whom the very word 'purity' is anathema, and who even stigmatise its practice as 'sex-inadequacy', holding that the human being is basically incomplete and maimed in the absence of actual sex experience.

(vi) Detailed attention is given to the *means* to be used in inculcating a positive love of purity. Those mentioned are :
  (*a*) Prayer.
  (*b*) Assiduous use of the Sacrament of Penance.
  (*c*) Frequent reception of Holy Communion.
  (*d*) The practice of devotion to Our Blessed Lady as Mother and Pattern of Purity.
  (*e*) The avoidance of dangerous reading, indecent scenic performances, bad company and bad talk, and other occasions of sin.

It will be seen at once that this positive pursuit of purity introduces us to the whole field of Christian asceticism, involving self-control and abnegation in many directions other than the purely sexual. This is a point of prime importance. It is morally impossible to remain pure, and still more to advance towards the positive perfection of the virtue, if one is unrestrained, self-indulgent and unmortified in all departments of life other than the sexual. In this matter true Christian asceticism is beyond all doubt the weapon of choice for the Christian, and it is vain to look for a substitute for this weapon.

(vii) The responsibility of sex-enlightenment is placed quite definitely on the shoulders of the *parents*. Definite and convincing reasons for this are assigned, and here again the Holy See's position is quite unassailable. It is, however, evident that Rome is not unaware of the fact that, in all too many cases, parents do not carry out their responsibility in this matter and that they are 'often unprepared and ill-equipped for their work as educators'. It is the principal purpose of this book to formulate some practical corollaries of this state of affairs.

It is then quite obvious that the Church knows her own mind on this subject very clearly, and has given detailed and definite expression to that mind on several occasions, especially in recent years.

III

MAIN GUIDING PRINCIPLES

As in all education generally, so particularly in this part of it, planning and procedure must be determined by *aim*. What, then, are we aiming at as educators? Surely, at the production of the true man and woman. The question at once arises: What *is* man? What should he be? What may he become? Unless this question is answered, fruitful and insightful education is impossible. And note that the question is not 'What is human intellect'? or 'What are the requirements of the 20th century'? or 'What is the socially acceptable citizen of contemporary England'? but 'What is Man'? The question is an enquiry about an organic *whole*, and it cannot be answered by reference to parts or aspects, or conventional expediencies. Moreover, it is a question which neither Parliament nor Government nor Ministry of Health nor Board of Education nor N.U.T. are competent to answer. That answer must be sought from one source, and one source only—from the Church of God. Now, however correct it may be as a philosophical abstraction, the Church teaches that the term 'rational animal' is not a full and adequate description of Man as he actually exists. Man is a rational animal unspeakably ennobled by divine grace, raised to the true sonship of the Father Who created him, destined to be a 'member of the household of God' through all the long reaches of eternity. This was the being, Man, as he came fresh from the hands of his Creator in the golden dawn of time. By sin indeed he fell from his high estate to that of a mere rational animal lacking that supernatural dignity which his nature was created to sustain. But by the Sacraments of the Church he is raised again to sonship and fellowship with God, and destined anew to an eternity of light in the gaze of his Father.

That is just the truth about Man, and it must be normative for everything which intimately concerns him. It is in his super-natural calling and destiny that the keystone to Man's wholeness is to be found. In the last resort, it is grace, and grace alone, which is able to hold our human complexity together in harmony and integration. No other force is adequate; there is a strife and a conflict in the inner recesses of human nature which can only be resolved by 'the high thoughts of the sons of God.' There is no mere rhetoric here, but a plain fact which is the very centre and heart of the Christian faith. Now the sex urge affects man as a whole; its dynamic is a principal component of the internal conflict which only the life of the Spirit is able to resolve. The Christian approach to sex must therefore be on a high level—the level of the man who is really *whole*, the man ennobled by his divine elevation and destiny. Consequently, any 'undenominational,' naturalistic treatment of the subject, which appeals to natural motives and values alone, and purports to effect integration without recourse to man's specifically spiritual nature, must be regarded as inadequate and *seriously* so. We do not claim that others must follow us in this view; we respect their evident good intentions, we applaud their high natural ideals, which are indeed the indispensable foundation for the crowning work of the spirit. But we have resources they wot not of, and we know with certainty that without calling upon those resources full human integration in this vital matter can never be achieved. A quotation from a contemporary comment on this subject will serve to illustrate at once the elevation of aim and yet the basic inadequacy of those who attack this problem with natural motives alone.

'Perhaps the main criticism that can be levelled against this publication is its almost complete scholastic isolation and neglect of the social forces involved as determinants of sexual attitudes and behaviour. The prefatory note refers to "the immediate problem presented by the increased number of young persons who fall victims to the special temptations and circumstances of wartime", and expresses the excellent hope that further efforts will be made "to bring such persons within the influence of the Youth Service". But there is no mystical quality to the phrase "youth service" which will enable it to conquer its environment. All sorts of social changes will be needed before sex education can yield its fullest fruits. The economic barriers to early marriage must go, and we must so conduct our society that millions of homes are not periodically broken up. Young people must be given some burning sense of social purpose, some feeling that they can be of real service to the community and be valued by it, some belief in a future for which it is worth while to sacrifice immediate sensual gratification. Sex education cannot thrive *in vacuo*. It must be sex education for a particular social setting'.

From Review of Govt. (B. of E.) Educational Pamphlet No. 119, 'Sex Education in Schools and Youth Organisations', in *Nature*, November 20th, 1943, page 582.

A 'burning sense of social purpose', a realisation of value and a face set bravely towards the future—these are all good, and very good, and yet not good *enough* for a real man, nor mighty enough to motivate that rigorous and penetrating training of the whole man which fits him for the arduous ascent of the holy mountain to the City of God.

IV

MISAPPREHENSIONS, INSUFFICIENCIES AND MISTAKES IN SEX EDUCATION

(*a*) **Knowledge and Conduct.**—Many persons active in this field are so obsessed with the woeful ignorance of the population at large on sex matters, that they have come to convince themselves that by banishing this ignorance they will have solved the problem and fulfilled all justice. This attitude is widespread and is implemented in practice by many who would not, after due reflection, maintain it in theory. Such a view completely loses sight of the 'wholeness-aspect' of the problem, and consequently rushes into a facile solution which is hopelessly inadequate, and which may indeed even aggravate the very condition it seeks to heal. Knowledge does *not* necessarily bring virtue in its train. I venture to be very emphatic on this point; if you are going to instruct the young on sex matters at all, you must do far more than merely instruct. The problem cannot be settled so easily, and it is unscientific in the highest degree to suppose that it can. Those, whoever they be, who wish to enter this field, must ask themselves: 'What have I to offer over and above mere physiological instruction; for if this is all I have to give, I had far better remain silent, at any rate so far as children are concerned'?

(*b*) **Biology in the Schools.**—Akin to the errors just mentioned is that which holds that *the* ideal and adequate solution to the whole problem is to be found in the introduction of biological teaching into the schools. It is my own view that at this particular epoch of our civilisation biology is a science of the first importance, and that a very strong case can be made out for its inclusion in school curricula, even at the expense of a good deal of the physics, chemistry and (dare I say it?) mathematics that is now taught. But I do not want to see it dragged into the syllabus as a mere convenience or cloak for sex teaching. Biology, if taught on its own merits as a science, as I believe it should be, is obviously of the greatest assistance in mediating instruction on the physiological aspect of sex and relating it coherently to the other manifestations of life. But physiological instruction is but

B

a part, and not the principal part nor the normative part, of sex enlightenment. Taken by itself, the teaching of biology would even result in a flagrant *non sequitur* in its impact on sex enlightenment. That the effect of this *non sequitur* is often not removed from the minds of adults whose approach to sex knowledge was made through biology is evidenced by a good deal of contemporary writing. I venture to illustrate this *non sequitur* by a condensed parody of the sort of biological teaching which I have in mind:—

'The unit of life is the cell, and the life of the cell is basically typical of all life. The higher forms of life are organised aggregations of many cells. As we go up the evolutionary series from amœba to Man, we find the same basic cell-life manifesting itself in different modalities and co-ordinating its activities with those of neighbouring cells with modified functions. As we ascend the evolutionary series, we find ever-increasing differentiation, but the series is continuous, and throughout it life is of the same basic character. At present, modern man stands at the head of the evolutionary series, he is its latest and most differentiated product. His life and nature are of the same character as those of the lower forms which preceded him, and from which he derived—he differs from the lower organisms not in kind but in degree only, his functions are more specialised. Just as life itself becomes more and more specialised as we ascend the evolutionary scale, so does that particular manifestation of life, which we call reproduction. The Amœba divides and multiplies itself by simple fission; Paramœcium sometimes gets tired of this, and two individuals blend and then separate again to continue their reproductive activity independently ; earth worms mate by bringing their sexual areas into apposition ; the male fish sheds its sex-product into the water and thus fertilises the female without the necessity of contact ; the frog sheds his product while clasping his mate, but without intromission ; in the mammal, there is more highly developed sexual congress with intromission, there is prolonged gestation, the young are born alive and are subject to parental or at least maternal care. All through the life-series we find the sexes coming together and reproducing their kind exuberantly. And you are just the same as them— your life is biologically continuous with theirs. BUT YOU MUSTN'T DO IT!' What wonder if the child is so puzzled that it doesn't even ask 'Why?' And if the question were put, what would the biologist, as a biologist, reply? Would his biological reply suffice to motivate and implement the prohibition ?

(*c*) **Natural Modesty and the Sense of Shame.**—We come on to a very complicated subject here, and one which merits far more attention and study than it has yet received. There is more than a tendency nowadays to regard both natural modesty and the sense of shame as the rank and twisted outgrowth of the strictness of Victorian convention and the hypocritical prudery of the 'hush-hush' policy. Now while it is quite true that convention and social habit can to a certain extent shape the framework within which natural modesty and the sense of shame will operate, it is surely false to suppose that these reactions are wholly acquired, or exclusively due to the impact of the social environment on the individual. Space does not permit of a full discussion here, but there is good evidence to support the conclusion that in natural modesty we have a disposition of an instinctive or inborn nature—a component of the natural equipment of Man's being. Nature seems to have made provision for the protection of the labile sex urge against undue, untimely, unwanted or unnatural stimulation. If it be so, this is by no means the only instance in which Nature counterpoises one dynamic with another opposed to it. From the whole analogy of autonomic nervous control, one would not expect the sex urge to be left exposed to explosive activation at the instance of any and every stimulus, however adventitious.

Now if natural modesty is a natural inborn provision for the protection of the sex urge, it is clearly a very misconceived form of sex-enlightenment which begins by breaking this natural modesty down. I believe that this is one of the considerations at the back of the Holy See's disapproval of the intimate discussion of these matters in public. It would be a mistake of superficiality to conclude from the self-assured mien of modern youth, that this natural modesty is lacking in them—inborn tendencies do not disappear so easily. Thus any form of sex-enlightenment which neglects this factor, fails to make provision for it, or misinterprets it, is hardly likely to be adequate.

(d) **Guilt and the Modern Psychologist.**—Closely allied to the foregoing topic is the attitude commonly taken up by the modern psychologist and psychiatrist to the question of guilt. In the treatment of neurotic disorders of a sexual origin or content, it is a commonplace that any attitude to the matter which heightens the sense of guilt in the patient simply aggravates the condition, and in many cases the psychiatrist judges it to be his part to clear the field of guilt right at the beginning of the case. Now there is a sense in which the sense of guilt is a hindrance to virtue rather than a help, but it is much to be feared that the matter is often handled in an altogether uncritical way, so that in the attempt to free the patient from 'pathological guilt', grave injury is inflicted on his moral sensitiveness, thus committing the error which is perhaps characteristic of this uncritical age, that of 'emptying out the baby with the bath'. I feel that this question calls for some attention here, since many agencies active in this field of sex-enlightenment have, on the advice of psychiatrists, gone over-far in their avoidance of anything likely to generate a feeling of guilt with regard to departures from right sex conduct. Very clear thinking is called for here. We must distinguish carefully between intellectually apprehended guilt connoted by the realization of actual moral imputability, and the emotional 'guilt' which normally accompanies such rational guilt, but which may all too easily become split off from it. The point may perhaps be illustrated by a consideration of the following three imaginary cases :—

(a) Mr. Jones, a well-connected and prominent man in a smallish country town, is discovered red-handed in some mean, despicable and shameful offence, for which he is subsequently convicted by the law. Consider Mr. Jones' state of mind at the moment of discovery. He knows he is guilty, his reason tells him clearly that he is responsible for the miserable crime which he knowingly, willingly and deliberately committed. In the sight of all his friends and associates the matter comes to light. An overwhelming emotion of shame rushes over him, his face reddens, he goes 'hot all over', he does not know where to look, he feels that he wants to sink into the earth, and hide himself from the accusing gaze of his fellow-men.

(b) Mr. Bloggs, a denizen of the London underworld, is caught red-handed and convicted for the very same crime which brought Mr. Jones to ruin. Bloggs knows he is guilty, he knows he has done wrong and will have to expiate it. But as he listens to the long roll of his previous convictions being read out in court, he feels little emotion. There was a time when he felt shame, but that was a long time ago ; and now he only feels annoyance that he has been unfortunate enough to get caught.

(c) Mr. Brown, a rising and ambitious young man, is asked out to a rather smart evening function. He is a little late in returning from business ; he dresses rapidly but with some care, and sets off for his evening's enjoyment. He enters the house, gives up hat and coat, shakes hands with his host and hostess, and is introduced to some of the smartly dressed people in the well-filled rooms. He sits down, and having 'hitched' his trouser-leg to do so, discovers that in his haste to dress he has only put on one sock, so that a six-inch expanse of bare leg and ankle are showing. The eyes of all in the room seem to be upon him, there is a smothered snigger somewhere, he turns furiously red, he goes 'hot all over', he dare look at no one, he wishes the lights would go out, or that he could sink into the earth out of sight—in short he feels an utter and complete worm. And yet he *knows* that he is guilty of nothing worse than working late and dressing in a hurry.

Reviewing these three cases, we see that in Jones we have real moral guilt and an emotional state which matches up and corresponds to it ; in Bloggs we have real moral guilt with no answering emotion ; while in Brown we have an intense wave of emotion almost entirely similar to that suffered by Jones, but with no real moral guilt at all.

The ordinary uninstructed person is often quite unable to distinguish between a rational conviction of real moral guilt, and a storm of 'emotional guilt.' In the normal case, of course, one should be a function of the other ; 'emotional shame and guilt' should only be present when there is real moral lapse to be guilty and ashamed about, and this emotion should be more or less intense according as the moral fault is more or less grave. But such nice adjustment is not always found, and in all too many individuals 'emotional guilt and shame' have been partly or even almost completely split off from any conscious rational backing, or at any rate exist in an intensity which is wildly disproportionate to the real guilt of the situation which evokes them. The causes of such disproportion are manifold, and the matter is too complex to deal with fully in the present book. But there can be little doubt that one of the causes of this lack of harmony and balance between the rational and emotional attitude of the individual is faulty or injudicious sex instruction. The whole matter is, in its own nature, so heavily charged with emotional factors, that we need to be very careful and judicious in injecting any further emotional dynamism into our instruction, our advice, our appeals, admonitions and warnings. Especially when one is endeavouring to assist a young person to conquer habitual sexual delinquency, an over-dose of the fear-guilt-shame emotion will be found to have an effect the reverse of that which is desired, and to render the case almost intractable.

We adults must be specially on our guard against the danger of 'projecting' our adult attitude on to juvenile minds and consciences incapable of sustaining such a load. This may quite easily happen, not infrequently with grave results, when some indecency or similar lapse, which, in the mind and con-science of the child is in the order of untidyness or disobedience, is visited with a degree of reprobation which would be suitable and justified if the same act had been committed by an adult. Grave moral fault is not too lightly to be assumed in one of tender years—far more often help and advice and forbearance are called for rather than severity or even punishment.

It is this inadvisability of unduly heightening the emotional potential of the matter that has led many to look askance at any attempt to put sex enlightenment on the high plane which is proper to it (as indicated in pp. 7–9 above), and to consider that the inculcation of a positive love and desire for purity cannot be effected without at the same time sowing the seeds of a pathological and distorted attitude to the whole matter. These folk do not seem to realise that there is all the world of difference between the sustaining emotions proper to high purpose and enthusiasm and the depressive emotions of fear, shame and guilt. In this reaction against emotion of any kind, the 'hard-boiled' school of sex-instructors even render themselves incapable of investing the subject with that essential dignity which its intimately human nature demands ; it is interesting to note how invincibly satisfied they are with the suitability and success of their methods, when one knows that their efforts have been received by their young audience with very mixed opinions.

Much more serious is it, when in the course of sex instruction or advice on sex matters, positive steps are taken to dispel all sense of guilt, or to explain away guilt as a resultant from a mere deviation from currently accepted social practice and convention. It would be easy to quote many instances in which this has been done, by well-intentioned but muddle-headed and uncritical folk, both by the spoken word and in print. Such a procedure is, of course, analogous to that of cutting off the head to cure the tooth-ache. In both cases the cure is efficacious ; one's teeth can't ache if one has lost one's head and one's teeth with it, one will no longer be troubled by guilt if one is fully convinced that there is nothing to feel guilty about, nor any law to break save that of one's own convenience in one's reaction to the social organism.

(e) 'They get to know anyhow'. How often has this remark been heard from those who take the lazy view that *ad hoc* sex enlightenment of the young is entirely unnecessary ? Unfortunately, in all too many cases, the remark is quite true ; in the absence of proper instruction, knowledge is picked up just *anyhow*. But this is obviously not good enough, it should be our aim to train our children in important matters, not just 'anyhow', but in the right way. It may sometimes be necessary to lick up muddy water from odd puddles, but it would be foolish to require people to do so when pure clear water from an untainted source was easily available.

It is true that young people in agricultural areas often become acquainted with all that it is necessary for them to know, without external intervention. But experience shows that this is far from being the case with the children of urban populations. Those who lack much experience in this matter would, I think, be greatly surprised if they knew the frequency with which quite gross misapprehensions regarding sex are found in otherwise well-educated adults ; while it is only those few who are consulted on such matters who realise how very damaging such misapprehensions may be and how far-reaching their effects on life, character and happiness. I have already indicated that, if sex instruction is given at all, it should be clear, accurate and complete within the limits of ordinary requirements—and I shall return to this point later. From this point of view alone, the *laissez faire* attitude of 'They get to know anyhow !' is condemned, to say nothing of the only too possible morally subversive effects of knowledge communicated from tainted sources. Pope Pius XII draws explicit attention to these dangers in his Allocution of 26 October, 1941.

(*f*) **'We got on all right without sex instruction in the past'.** This objection must receive serious attention, for the implication underlying it is that the more urgently we represent sex instruction as a vital need, the more clearly we stigmatise past methods as grossly insufficient and malign the generations which have preceded us. In the mouths of some, this objection has almost the force of representing the advocacy of sex instruction as an attack on the Church itself, since in all ages since the dawn of the Christian era the Church has had at her disposal and in her keeping everything which is required for man's essential well-being. To deal with this objection fully would entail an essay on the evolution of civilisation, with particular reference to its later stages, which would scarcely be in place in a work of this compass. Here however are a few brief points tending to show that our present epoch has its own special requirements, which did not exist, or existed to a far smaller extent, until a generation or two ago :—

(i) About 80 per cent. of our population is in urban areas, and is consequently shut off to a large extent from the observation of natural processes. This urbanisation is of comparatively recent growth, and has raised a whole host of problems that did not formerly exist.

(ii) Our young people are growing up into a world which has lost its *moral standards*. Former ages did not, perhaps, always greatly excel our own in the practice and observance of morality, but the standard and obligation of morality were still everywhere recognized. In former days men sinned indeed, but they knew they were sinning and acknowledged it ; they knew that they were doing wrong, while to-day the recognition of a sharp distinction between right and wrong has almost vanished. It may have been hypocritical ; it may have been logically indefensible, but it is still a fact that the community as a whole

30 years ago reprobated a great many things which to-day it tolerates and even regards as normal.

(iii) The impact of religion on public and social life has enormously declined. In the days when there were popular celebrations of the recurrent feasts of the Church, when mystery and morality plays were common, when judges, lawyers, professors, students, officials and trade guilds made public profession of their religious faith, when processions and pilgrimages had not yet become things to be scoffed at, the Church's influence went deep into the innermost fibres of national, public, social, local, and family life. Long after leaving school the citizen was subject to the teaching impact of life itself as it was conducted in all its aspects in the contemporary scene. Nowadays the child leaves school at 14, and only in few cases thereafter does he find the fabric of life in which he is enmeshed, morally educative. All this applies with particular force to courtship, marriage and the relations between the sexes generally. Obviously more explicit formation and instruction are called for when the individual has to maintain his own standard in an environment which has lost all standards.

The country as a whole has become familiarized with the fact that the extent of juvenile delinquency presents us with a major problem, but certain types of juvenile breakdown are never reported in the Press, and indeed in many instances escape the possibility of any intervention on the part of the legal authorities. It is by no means as rare as most people think for a young girl of 15 or even less to become pregnant or to contract venereal disease as a first infection, and I am informed that in recent years such cases have become even less rare, causing serious alarm to those in touch with such matters.

(iv) Urbanisation, travel facilities, large-scale commercialised amusements, and the general shrinkage of the family unit, have largely destroyed the education and formative effect of family life for all except the younger children.

(v) In elementary education the stress seems to have been laid on mere instruction, and the minimum of informed attention has been given to training and character formation. The role of religion as an integral part, and indeed the key-stone, of education has been lost sight of. Without it, elementary education has proved utterly unable to equip our children with ethical motives and definite standards of conduct adequate for a stable life. We have become the creatures of custom and convention rather than of conviction ; and our customs and conventions have been revolutionized in a generation, and in a disastrous sense, under the onslaught of a sensational amoral Press and infidel propaganda. The short history of compulsory education might perhaps be summarised by saying that knowledge has grown, and with it a feverish hunger for the good things to which knowledge gives access, but without a sense of values by which alone these good things can be rightly integrated into the complexity of human life as a whole.

(vi) Modern popular literature, both periodical and in book form, the stage, the screen and even the wireless have all played their part in the generation of an atmosphere and an attitude to moral questions which our fathers and mothers find very surprising and which our grandparents would not have tolerated. Children are nowadays allowed access to reading matter, entertainments and other stimulants of their imagination, such as they would have been authoritatively shielded from a generation ago. Much indeed that is beautiful, noble and uplifting has been produced on stage, screen and radio ; but even in some quite superior productions there have been all too many instances of a highly-skilled and deliberate titillation of undesirable emotions, carried out by suggestion rather than by direct means, and often effected with great artistry and considerable psychological skill. It is a far cry from the pantomime once a year at Christmas of a generation ago, to the modern visit once or twice a week to the cinema.

The above has not been written in the spirit of a *laudator temporis acti*, but in order to make the point that times *have* changed, and that the training methods of bygone generations need considerable revision if they are to equip our young folk adequately to withstand the modern stream of solicitation and allurement with which their immature affections are all too early wooed.

V

ADOLESCENCE AND SEX ADJUSTMENT

The emergence of the man or woman from the child is a phase of vast importance and fascinating interest. That emergence is, of course, a gradual process, but it proceeds with particular rapidity during the period of pubescence, while the reproductive equipment of the individual is coming to maturity. Though these pages are designed to deal particularly with the sex aspect of this phase, it must be remembered that sexual changes are by no means the only changes taking place at this time. There is a dawning realization of self-value, of one's own dynamic potentialities ; there is a new gravity and a new sense of responsibility ; new vistas and avenues open up—it is a time of endeavour, of golden hopes, of lofty ideals, of solemn self-dedication, of eager service and ready loyalties.

It is easy enough to see how fitting it is that Nature should have provided for the emergence of these psychological and spiritual factors just at the time when the physiological possibility of mating and parenthood first arises. Keeping our eye on the 'wholeness-aspect' of the matter, we find the instinctive drive of sex lying at the core and centre of a most complex and important phase of human development. Quite apart from our allegiance to any particular school of psychological thought, we can easily recognise that a failure (from whatever cause) on the part of the conscious personality to cope with the newly-emerging elements of sex-experience is almost certain to maim the personality and to prevent its harmonious integrated development.

No apology, therefore, should be needed, nor should one incur the reproach of pan-sexualism or sex-obsession, in maintaining that adequate sex-adjustment is of *immense* importance. If this is secured, the other and intrinsically more worth-while factors of personality may easily be built into place. If this be not secured, the personality is bound to have a stormy passage, and growth is certain to be retarded or distorted—not infrequently to a disastrous extent. Psychiatrists, and others doing similar work, are constantly being brought into contact with cases of breakdown and inadequacy directly or indirectly traceable to a failure on the part of the individual to cope with the demands of the sex instinct on a sound and healthy basis. Stages in the development of the personality, which should have occurred sweetly and naturally during childhood, have to be brought about in the maladjusted adult by laborious and painful efforts, working against half a life-time of mental and emotional habit and experience. Through similar causes, marriages are often ruined and family life greatly prejudiced. In sum, there is a vast amount of preventible human misery and inefficiency caused by the prevailing failure to handle this important subject as it should be handled.

Although the whole matter focuses itself up very sharply during adolescence, it would be a great mistake to suppose that the problem of suitable sex-enlightenment can be solved by a study of the adolescent period alone. By a study of adolescence we can indeed see the nature and importance of the whole matter more clearly, possibly because it is at adolescence that the ill-effects of maladjustment begin to make themselves most strikingly manifest. But while this intensive period of accelerated formation and consolidation merits our closest attention, the fact must never be lost sight of that a satisfactory adolescence is to a large extent a function of a satisfactory childhood. Adolescence does not mark the beginning of sex-adjustment, but its virtual completion. Adolescent problems and mal-adjustments are, in the main, emergents from childhood training and experience. It is for this reason that in his Allocution of 26 October, 1941, Pope Pius XII so wisely insists on the paramount importance of right training methods during early childhood ; and it is for this reason that we shall later draw the inescapable conclusion that it is to the *parents* that the duty and responsibility of sex-enlightenment naturally fall.

It is easy to see that the hitherto prevailing method (or rather, complete lack of method) is much more likely to produce a *dissociation* of the personality than an integration. When a child who asks where the new baby came from is told that a stork brought it, or that it came in the doctor's attaché case, that is an untruth. It will eventually be found out to be an untruth—if indeed it is ever believed at all. And when this happens, we may suppose a process in the child's mind something like the following : 'Daddy and Mummie always speak the truth. They say it's wrong not to speak the truth. They punish me if I tell a lie. They have never told me anything bu the truth before. But about this baby-business they have told me something which isn't true. I wonder why ? This baby-business doesn't seem to follow the ordinary rules'. Again, when parents blush and stammer and look awkward when asked questions about sex, the child feels that the whole thing is different— it doesn't follow the ordinary rules. This is even more the case if the inquisitive child is rebuked, hushed-down or told not to be 'rude'—for why is it rude to ask a perfectly simple question about something with regard to which one is curious ? Again, if a small child commits some infantile misbehaviour or indecency and it is at once visited with the same degree of moral reprobation as might be suitable for an adult guilty of corresponding actions, the child simply cannot understand it, and again the whole matter is relegated to that queer department in which babies, and micturition and the exposure of one's own chubby person and the difference between Jimmy and his little sister Jenny are huddled together in complete isolation from the rest of the mental contents, since they are *different*, they don't obey the ordinary rules, they're in some undefined way wrong, disgusting, discreditable.

Thus it comes about that these things are not 'apperceived'— there is no conscious integration of these items with the other elements of organised knowledge—they are not coped with in terms of reality-concepts. *And yet they are very much there* ! Since the reality-category of consciousness cannot cope with them, there is set up an extra-conscious scheme for them—often wildly irrational—and to this separated 'island' system of mind becomes aggregated a whole series of important experiences and ideas and affects as the organism develops. This picture comes so near to Freudian 'repression' that the difference does not matter much for our immediate practical purposes.

VI
SOME ILL-EFFECTS OF MALADJUSTMENT

(i) It will easily be seen that the faulty attitude to sex outlined in the two preceding paragraphs tends to mental dissociation. It is obvious that such conditions may cause serious dissociative disorders ; such disorders range from the all too common chronic anxiety neurosis to the gravest forms of mental breakdown. It is true that grave mental disorder probably requires other constitutional predispositions, but nevertheless these predispositions might remain only latent in the presence of sound sexual hygiene.

(ii) The individual who has not succeeded in bringing the question of sex into rational relationship with the rest of his psychic life is often an easy prey to emergency situations and seductions.

(iii) Since mind has not learned to deal rationally with these matters, they are handled irrationally. This often results in the development of an exaggerated strictness and puritanism in the matter, which could not be justified in reason and which are supported by an infantile emotional scheme containing elements scarcely distinguishable from superstition, magic and totemism. In such cases often enough the individual assumes a load of obligation which neither the physical, psychological nor spiritual nature of man is adapted to bear.

(iv) By way of reaction against a load of obligation which threatens to bring life to a standstill, the individual may throw off all checks and plunge into an orgy of indulgence—casting out the devil of scrupulosity by the Beelzebub of debauchery.

(v) If both these dangers are escaped, the maladjusted individual will probably take up the imperfect attitude dictated by the modern materialistic environment ; or will at least obtain wrong and distorted information from some undesirable source.

(vi) Unhappiness and grave difficulties in marriage, leading in some cases to separation or divorce, and in other cases to seriously impaired health, may be caused by a faulty attitude to, or ignorance regarding, sex matters.

(vii) A faulty attitude on this question on the part of the

parents is *very* likely to be transmitted to the offspring. Psychiatrists are only too familiar with cases of pathological inhibition, phobias, fears, anxieties, delinquency, and character deviations of all descriptions, whose origin can be tracked back to family relationships arising from faulty attitudes on the part of maladjusted parents. The importance of this prolific cause of psychological trouble and breakdown can hardly be exaggerated.

VII

'A NATION OF THE EMOTIONALLY IMMATURE'

In a recent article, Dr. E. B. Strauss* pointed out that the emancipation at the age of 14 from all further formative and educational control which is the lot of the vast majority of our rising generation, must result in the formation of a proletarian class characterized by their emotional immaturity. Technical and professional instruction indeed goes forward after the age of 14, but no really educative and cultural influence is at work enabling the emotional factors of life, and the values attaching to them, to be brought into integral relationship with the life of the mind and the world of ideas. A 'thing which has struck me very forcibly', he says, 'and which never ceases to astonish and surprise me, is the dramatic change to the total personality, body and mind, which occurs at puberty. If a person's schooling terminates with the advent of puberty, he is for ever condemned to remain uneducated ; the things of the mind will be a closed book to him, and cultural values remain meaningless mysteries'.

In man, the life of the emotions and the life of the mind are meant to marry ; if the union does not take place, both remain stunted, dwarfed, immature. Perhaps we have now become discerning enough to see that a large section of our nation was in fact seriously immature—we were in the deadly instability of a largely immature people struggling to preserve a way of life that had waxed to its maturity through many centuries of gentle and stormy growth. The war has made us grow up a little, though scarcely enough as yet. But it is enough to scan the leaders and the headlines of our pre-war popular daily Press, to be shocked at the trivial decadence from which we have been so rudely awakened. We are faced with an immense educational task, right now and in the years of strenuous peace towards which we gaze. That education must go far beyond mere

---

* 'The Physiological Case for Post-Primary Education,' *Time & Tide*, 14 Aug., 1943, page 663.

instruction, and reach right down to the depths in which man is welded into a real dynamic unity. And it must invoke those spiritual agencies which alone are adequate to effect this mighty welding. Real training and character formation must needs grapple with the affective or emotional side of man's life. And at the dynamic centre of that affective life we find the sex urge in all its complexity, sending out its feelers and connections to all other parts. We may deprecate the importance of actual sex experience as we will, and it is clear that it looms far too large in contemporary thought, but it nevertheless remains certain that real emotional stability will never be achieved if the sex component of the affective life is left in a state of disorder, disintegration, immaturity, disharmony.

Attention has been drawn to this phase of the matter, in order to bring out the fact that the securing of adequate and normal sex-adjustment has implications which go far beyond the avoidance of sexual misdemeanour and the contraction of venereal disease.

VIII

HOW, WHEN, AND BY WHOM SHOULD SEX ENLIGHTENMENT BE EFFECTED ?

Having cleared the ground to a certain extent, we are now able to attack the problem in a somewhat more detailed manner, with the aim of arriving at constructive proposals. Enough has already been said to show that sex enlightenment does not necessarily come about automatically without any steps being taken in the matter and that this important vital adjustment should not be left to the vagaries of chance. It follows therefore that sex enlightenment must be effected deliberately, methodically and correctly by the right agency and at the right time. Three main questions at once arise : (i) what exact method should be adopted in sex enlightenment ? (ii) at what age should it be effected ? (iii) by whom should it be carried out ? It will easily be seen that the answers to the first two questions depend largely on the answer to the third. Now the answer to the third question is supplied quite clearly and unequivocally by Pope Pius XII in his Allocution of 26/10/41. The Pope says quite definitely that the duty and responsibility of sex enlightenment rests on the parents. A brief study of some of the many reasons for which this duty devolves on parents will throw a good deal of light on the manner in which it should be carried out and the age at which it should be effected.

Why the Parents ?

(i) The parents have the primary duty and inalienable right of educating or directing the education of their own children.

(ii) The requirements of the individual regarding sex knowledge obviously bear a close relationship to the individual's age. Even the minor curiosities of the quite small child have to be duly met, but it would evidently be entirely out of place to satisfy such infantile curiosity by a complete exposition of the whole subject. The information should be imparted little by little throughout almost the whole of the child's intelligent life. If mediated in this gradual, almost unnoticed fashion, sex knowledge will be take for granted in a very matter-of-fact way with the minimum injection of emotional content. But it is not the chronological age of the child which determines the moment at which successive items of information should be imparted and successive stages of training carried out. Children of the same chronological age differ very widely in their needs in this respect. It is obviously the good parent who is best able to mark and note those stages of personality growth which call for increased knowledge and make the child receptive to a further stage of training. The parent has a wider choice of times and circumstances, and his knowledge of the child's character and probable reactions is (or should be) greater than that of the school teacher. The parent is consequently in a position, not only to intervene at the right stage in the child's development, but also to choose the best time for doing so, to avoid unsuitable times or circumstances and to exploit some suitable phase of family life for the purpose.

(iii) Sex enlightenment carried out in the right way by good parents is, by that very fact, placed in its right setting and relationship—that of the Catholic family. The whole subject then becomes invested with its proper dignity and is placed on the high level to which it really belongs, that of the sacred and intimate things which belong to family life and are but sparingly shared with outsiders. From the lips of a good and devoted father or mother, the story of life will bring to the child a sense of beauty and reverent wonder as a permanent possession, so that he will come to regard any subsequent cheapening of the topic with resentment and disgust.* In a very real sense it is

---

* A good illustration of the delicate and even beautiful way in which such instruction can be carried out is given on pages 55-62 of 'Never No More', a novel by Maura Laverty, published by Messrs Longmans. The account is somewhat idealised, and few parents or relations will attain the high level of artistry shown in the instruction of Miss Laverty's 'Gran' ; indeed each individual case calls for special treatment. But the passage quoted shows how easily and naturally and beautifully the necessary knowledge may be imparted under conditions of mutual confidence, understanding and affection between child and adult.

only the parents who are able to pass on the whole truth and the whole wonderful meaning of the 'facts of life'—any others who, for one reason or another, have to undertake the task labour under a great disadvantage precisely because they are not the parents of the child whom they are instructing.

(iv) Such a method should greatly facilitate the due emergence of an adult attitude to marriage, parenthood and family life— there are those who think that the lack of such an attitude is a canker at the heart of our national life, and such a view is by no means without justification.

(v) If parents carry out this duty, due account can be taken of the brothers and sisters of the child being instructed. These may be younger or older, or both ; co-ordination is called for, due reticence has to be inculcated, and this can scarcely be provided for in extra-parental tuition.

(vi) Since in the good Catholic family the hearth and the altar are so intimately joined, the religious and spiritual values without which sex-adjustment can never be adequately achieved, are easily and naturally brought into their right relationship with personal aims and conduct in the matter.

(vii) The parents, far better than others, are able to provide at the right moment and in the right way for special contingencies in their children's lives, such as

(a) Going to school
(b) Going to boarding school
(c) Leaving home
(d) Commencing business or work
(e) Special dangers and temptations
(f) Association with the other sex, dances, courtship, etc.
(g) Preparation for marriage
(h) Fostering a religious or priestly vocation, if lads or girls themselves feel drawn to such a life.

(viii) If sex enlightenment is carried out step by step through-out the child's life in the family, it is to the parent that the child will naturally turn in any perplexity, obscurity or danger which may beset him, *and he can turn to no one better.*

In the foregoing, I have presupposed good Catholic parents, a good Catholic home, and normal responsive children. This is certainly a somewhat idealised state of affairs and it may be feared that such ideal conditions are but rarely realised in our jangled and disorientated modern world. 'It is easy enough', it might be objected, 'to show how sex enlightenment should be carried out by the perfect parent in respect of the perfect child, but how is this to help the ordinary, very far from perfect, father or mother, dealing, not with the ideal child of the copy-book maxim, but with those dynamic bundles of wayward impulsiveness which are real, actual flesh-and-blood children?' The answer, surely, is that ideals are not useless just because they are not easy of realisation in actual practice. It seems to me that it is most important that we should have before our eyes a very clear idea of what is ideal, normal, correct, perfect—only thus shall we be able to examine existing practice with constructive insight. In other words, if we have no standard or criterion of what is the best, criticism must necessarily be aimless and largely unfruitful.

IX

THE PARENTS' FAILURE

We descend from the realm of ideals with something of a bump, when we are forced to admit that, as a matter of fact, most parents do *not* fulfil their duty in this respect. And, if we are honest, we shall have to admit that there is very little prospect that the majority of parents *will* fulfil this duty in the near future —unless indeed such influences can be brought to bear on parents as to produce in them a change of heart of which there is very little sign at present.

That in the large majority of cases sex enlightenment is mediated to the children through agencies other than that of the parents, I do firmly believe to be the case at present. Unfortunately statistics on this point are not available, though some months ago proposals were put forward for initiating a pilot statistical survey to throw further light on this question. In the absence of statistics, one has to rely on general impressions, and on a summation of the evidence afforded by such cases as come within one's own experience, or upon which reports are available. All this leads in my own case to the conviction that, in most instances, parents are not instructing their offspring in sex matters. Very little evidence favouring the contrary view has come under my notice. The recent Board of Education Pamphlet on Sex Education* indeed refers to defaulting parents in more moderate terms as 'a substantial proportion', but I am strongly of the opinion that the *majority* of children in this country at present do not receive adequate sex enlightenment from their parents. There is little reason to believe that there is any considerable difference between Catholic and non-Catholic parents in this respect. One has no means of assessing the proportions in which this failure exists in parents of different classes, social and educational levels, professions, occupations,

---

* Educational Pamphlet No. 119, London, H.M. Stationery Office, 1943. 6d.

districts, etc., but one is struck with the large number of otherwise good parents, even among those educationally well-equipped for this duty, such as doctors, who fail to instruct their children in this important matter. Even when specifically urged to carry out this duty, very many parents show themselves decidedly unwilling, and anxious to pass the task over to someone else.

We must also recognise that, quite apart from defaulting parents who are otherwise perfectly qualified and suitable to instruct their children on this subject, there are very many parents whose own faulty psychological attitude to the whole topic is such as substantially to unfit them for this work—the emotional tension engendered by an attempt to give such instruction to their own children would largely defeat the very purpose for which the instruction was given. Such cases are indeed abnormal and should not form the basis of a sound sex pedagogy ; but these abnormal emotional conditions in the home are met with much more frequently than most people would suspect, and must be taken serious account of. To attempt an explanation of this general failure and unwillingness would involve a lengthy discussion of the cultural, social, psychological and religious characteristics of our times, and I therefore have no intention of embarking here on an enquiry as to causes of this reluctance. The facts must be enough for us, and we shall be faced with a task sufficiently formidable in considering the practical reactions which these facts must involve if a remedy is to be provided.

If the foregoing is true, it will be seen that our problem is concerned mainly with three groups of individuals :

(i) The present generation of parents, who are not giving their own children sex-enlightenment, and who, in most cases, did not receive it from their own parents.

(ii) Family-emancipated adolescents (i.e. the next generation of parents) who have not received sex instruction from their parents, and who are now most unlikely so to receive it.

(iii) Children still under school and family control, who ought to be receiving parental sex guidance, but who are not in fact receiving it, and probably will not receive it in the future unless a very widespread change is brought about.

X

TRAINING FOR PARENTHOOD

The first group mentioned above, viz., the present generation of parents, are for many reasons very difficult of access for training purposes. Indeed the only universal channel of communication with them is the pulpit and this is a means of instruction particularly ill-adapted for the purposes we now have in view. It is true that most parents will very readily listen to advice on this subject, and that very many are anxious to become equipped to carry out their duty towards their children in this respect. Possibly such bodies as the newly-formed Catholic Parents' Association and the Catholic Council for Family and Population will be able to do something towards supplying this obvious need. There can be little doubt that the times call for the immediate establishment of courses of expert lectures on this and other aspects of family-craft. Such a conclusion is surely warranted by the words of Pope Pius XII's Allocution of 26 October, 1941, in which he refers to the Encyclical *Divini Illius Magistri* of his illustrious predecessor, pointing out that Pius XI 'went on regretfully to observe that parents are often unprepared or ill-equipped for their work as educators. Accordingly . . . in the name of Christ he exhorted all pastors of souls "to use every means by catechism and instruction, by word of mouth and in widely published writings, to ensure that Christian parents are well instructed both in general *and in particular* (italics ours) regarding their duties in the religious, moral, and civic education of their children' ".

But it is evident that some time must elapse before such courses of instruction as I have suggested reach more than a small proportion of Catholic parents, and that even among those whom such courses do reach there will be many who will be unwilling actually to implement the advice given them, and anxious to pass the task of instructing their children on to other hands. In other words, if we address ourselves to existing parents alone, it will be a very long time before we achieve a generation of parents who are substantially fulfilling their duty regarding this aspect of their children's upbringing. Since it is clear from the terms of Pius XII's Allocution that we are urged to secure the speedy establishment of such a generation of parents, our attention is insistently drawn to the second group mentioned on page 26, viz., the family-emancipated adolescents, who neither have received, nor are now likely to receive sex-enlightenment from their parents. This group is on the threshold of parenthood—they are the parents of the immediate future. They form a group which we cannot afford to neglect, they have to be equipped for their future duties as parents, and the conclusion seems to be inescapable that this is only practicable by extra-parental instruction. Previously to the war, by far the greater part of this group were effectively beyond the reach of any further educative influence ; the establishment of Youth Organisations, Clubs, Pre-Service Training Corps, etc., has since brought a large proportion (though by no means all) back within reach of training agencies.

We come finally to the third group mentioned on page 26, that of the children of school age who are not at present receiving and who are most probably not destined to receive sex-enlightenment from their parents, unless indeed a great change of attitude is brought about among the latter. A certain proportion of these children will be provided for, if a campaign to encourage parents to follow the advice of Pius XII is undertaken with some success. But, seeing that such a campaign has not yet begun*, it seems only prudent to conclude that a large number of these children, and indeed the greater part of them, are likely to pass through childhood and adolescence to adult life before we have succeeded in raising up a generation of parents who substantially carry out their duties in this respect.

Now it is in regard to this group, of children still at school and effectively under family influence and control, that the biggest difficulties are likely to arise in connection with sex teaching, and the biggest differences of opinion are likely to show themselves with regard to the best methods to adopt. Few would question the desirability, propriety and indeed necessity of providing instructional facilities and even collective instruction for parents who stand in need of it. Most would concede that adolescents whose requirements in this matter have not been met should not be allowed to pass on into adult life with inadequate knowledge of this important matter ; and here again some suitable form of collective treatment may be found necessary as a *partial* solution to the problem (though I shall later mention the reasons for my strong conviction that, in the nature of the case, certain aspects of the matter can never be successfully handled in the collective treatment either of children or adolescents, but call for individual treatment).† But there are very obvious difficulties in the way of securing that children of school age who should be receiving guidance from their parents in this

---

* Happily the issue of a Joint Pastoral Letter on this important subject by the Archbishops and Bishops of England and Wales has already made this remark somewhat out of date.

† In most cases (though by no means in all) the adolescent may be presumed to be acquainted with the elementary physiological facts concerning sex. It may, however, be necessary, in private interview, to make sure that this knowledge is correct and adequate. When this has been ensured, it will be easy to proceed to the collective handling of such topics connected with this subject as are suitable for public discussion, in the manner suggested at the beginning of the last page of the Joint Pastoral of April, 1944, where mention is made of the value of organisations of adolescents as a means of building up a generation of parents which will fulfil 'their duties in the religious, moral and civic education of their children'.

matter, but who are not in fact receiving it, should be duly provided for. The nature of some of these difficulties emerges at once from a consideration of the reasons given on pages 23–25 for holding that the parent is the natural agency for mediating this knowledge. Although it should be clear that full sex-adjustment cannot be expected to be achieved as early as the expiration of the primary school period, and that therefore the responsibility for achieving it can never be laid wholly on the primary school authorities, yet the question arises whether partial guidance can be furnished by the primary school, and if so, how much, when, and by what method—always keeping in mind the fact that we are dealing with those children for whom the school feels responsibility in default of the parents, or in regard to whom the parents wish to transfer their responsibility to the school. In order to carry this enquiry a stage further, a short reference must first be made to certain important differences in the requirements of young children and adolescents respectively.

XI

THE CHILD AND THE ADOLESCENT

Normal pre-adolescent curiosity in the matter of sex is substantially of the same character as the curiosity about other indifferent things manifested at this stage. When the child asks 'Daddy, why does the engine go ''puff-puff'' ?', an answer is given in simple mechanical terms, and the child is satisfied. Similarly, in a question as to the way in which babies come into the world, it is in the 'mechanics' of the matter that the child is interested, and if the process is explained in terms adapted to the questioner's years, curiosity is satisfied and the matter subsides naturally. This interest in the *process* rather than in the *fact* with its psycho-social implications is perhaps illustrated by the well-known story of the nurse who said to the little boy : 'A stork has brought you a dear little baby sister. Wouldn't you like to see it ?' 'No', replied the boy, 'but I'd like to see the stork'. At this stage, very little, if any, emotion attaches to the subject and it is handled in a very ordinary matter-of-fact way—indeed a normal child will rapidly become bored with the subject if the answers to his question are prolix.

But at puberty the whole subject becomes heavily invested with emotional factors. It is no longer a mere biological process in which the child is mildly interested from outside. It has become something close-up, something highly personal, something affecting the very depths of the self in a manner never before experienced, something so new as to appear unique, so that the adolescent is prone to lose sight of the fact that others have passed, and are passing through the same phase.

I have already pointed out (on pages 17, 22) that the phase of puberty brings with it much more than the mere physiological onset of sex maturity. Indeed one knows of many cases in which the years of adolescence, dynamic and full of change as they are, have contained but a minimum conscious preoccupation with sex matters, and surely this is as it should be. But adolescence makes tremendous claims on the vital resources of the individual, physiological, psychological and moral. Especially in the male, the personality-shaping process of adolescence takes widely varying and sometimes very puzzling forms. It is early in some, and late in others. In some it seems to occur almost overnight, in others it is protracted over several years. At this labile stage of his development, the adolescent is often an enigma to himself and largely isolated from everyone else. From almost all points of view it seems unwise in most cases to delay the communication of knowledge about the simple essential facts of reproduction to this stage. There seems to be considerable risk of provoking an emotional storm just at a time when the emotions are, as it were, having a hard struggle to consolidate themselves on other fronts. It may involve a quite unnecessary and possibly very exhausting and disorganising tax on emotional resources that are already strained to the uttermost.

In parenthesis, in this connection one is borne to reflect on the fact that it is during the time of puberty, or at least before adolescence has been completed, that we commonly submit our youth to fateful examination ordeals on which the whole future course of their lives may largely depend. One wonders if the resources of the late adolescent, already strained by the processes of physiological and psychological maturation, are really equal to the additional burden of prolonged and very intensive study for the finals of university examinations, medical qualification, etc. It is certainly the case that an intercurrent emotional crisis at this time, such as keenly felt bereavement or a love affair, has very often proved to be the precipitating cause of a breakdown having crippling effects extending over many years. Perhaps we may some day find it wise to introduce a 'Land Year' or a year of light occupation in the active professional sphere, before the year of final intensive preparation closing in its grim orgy of examinations.

With these thoughts in mind, many are nowadays urging that sex-education should take place before puberty. I suggest

that it is important to make a clear distinction here, between
mere elementary physiological instruction and the mediation
of more advanced knowledge of the social and personal implications of the sex instinct.   Quite a strong case seems to be made
out for the view that the elementary physiological facts of the
matter should be in the child's possession before the onset of
puberty, but it should also be clear that there are many considerations affecting this matter to which the child's mind will
not be responsive until a considerably later phase.   Consequently,
if, in default of the parents, elementary pre-pubertal instruction
has to be undertaken in the schools, a corresponding provision
for the guidance of youth must be made within the framework
of the vastly extended Youth Service which is envisaged.   It
should be clear that the whole of the training should be designed
in such a way as to fit young folk to carry out their duty, when
they eventually become parents, by undertaking the formation and
instruction of their own children.   All this will entail a great deal
of work, *and the expert training of suitable persons to engage on
such work*.   I fear that it is only too true that the great majority
of parents are not fulfilling their duty with respect to the sex-
education of their children, and am thus forced to the conclusion
that non-parental provision must be made, at least until a
suitably instructed new generation of parents emerges.   But
I emphatically disagree with those who seem to suppose that
the provision of an adequate substitute for parental instruction
is an easy matter.   Surely everything that has been said on
pp. 23–25 bears this out !   The fact is almost always lost sight
of that if once this field of sex conduct and responsibility is
activated in the adolescent mind by external instruction, a
demand will at once arise for answers by the instructing agency
to all sorts of perplexities and problems of a personal nature
which do not lend themselves to public discussion or collective
treatment.   In the ideal case, such questions would be answered
by the parent, but, since so many parents neglect the whole
matter, the questions usually never get addressed to them.   But
they come tumbling out if the topic so shyly eschewed by the
parents is suitably handled by someone else.   I believe therefore
that in any youth organisation which handles this matter, the
individual responsible for it must be prepared to act, not as
instructor only, but as guide and counsellor as well.   In Chapter
XIV of this book I give a number of hints and suggestions for
the benefit of those who may be called upon to engage in this
work ;   much of what is said in that chapter ought to be of use
to parents as well.   A fairly general reaction among those who
read that chapter when it was circulated in typescript for their
comments was a recognition of the fact that those who engage

in this work stand in need of a *more thorough and extensive training* than has hitherto been looked on as necessary. In the present book I can hardly do more than indicate the necessity of such training and point out that facilities for it hardly seem to exist as yet.

Whatever decisions are come to with regard to the most desirable and suitable time to effect the sex-enlightenment of normal children, we have to remember that circumstances and special needs alter cases. The idea of mentioning venereal disease and deviations from normal sex conduct in instructions to young children is highly repugnant. It would seem to mar and besmirch the dignity and beauty of the whole matter in the child's mind. And yet in certain districts the prevalence of promiscuity and the incidence of venereal disease in girls of under 16, and the lamentable conditions to which boys are sometimes subjected within a few weeks of leaving school to start work, may force one, however unwillingly, to make special instructional provision which should never have been rendered necessary. The general rule to follow in this regard is that education and formation should be such as to equip the pupil to meet the conditions which will impinge on him immediately the educative process is finished.

XII

SEX EDUCATION IN THE SCHOOL

It must first of all be pointed out that the local Bishop concerned is alone the competent authority for deciding whether the parents' failure is to be made good in Catholic schools, and, if so, what kind of instructional procedure should be adopted. What now are the principles which must govern the matter, if it is decided that in default of parental instruction and guidance, school instruction shall be resorted to, either generally or in some particular locality ?

Private individual instruction by a suitable teacher, authoritatively approved, acting with the parents' consent 'in loco parentis', appears to raise no difficulty beyond that of providing suitable and adequate training for the instructor. Whether such a procedure is here and now practicable, in large Catholic elementary schools for instance, I do not know, since I have had little experience of the administration of such institutions. Certainly I know of one large school in which it is done regularly, and I know of no decisive reasons which would prevent its adoption in other similar schools. Whether it is practicable by means of such individual instruction and guidance to provide for *all* the child's requirements in this matter, is a question which may be discussed later. But a single short interview with each child, in which those matters are simply explained which are better not handled in public, appears to be well within the range of practicability.

Class Instruction. In developing this subject further we are bound to come up against the questions : (i) Is class instruction in sex matters ever allowable ? (ii) If so, is it advisable, and to what extent ? So much misapprehension exists on this point, that I must treat it at some length and endeavour to make perfectly clear what the position is with regard both to allow-ability and advisability. The relevant document is the Encyclical of Pope Pius XI *Divini illius Magistri* of 31 December, 1929 ; and in that Encyclical the sentence which has the most direct reference to the point now under discussion is, in its Latin form, as follows : 'Passim enim bene multi et stulte et periculose eam tenent provehuntque educandi rationem, quae sexualis putide dicitur, cum iidem perperam sentiant, posse se, per artes mere naturales et quovis amoto religionis pietatisque praesidio, adolescentibus a voluptate et luxuria praecavere, scilicet hos omnes, nullo sexus discrimine, vel publice, lubricis initiando instruendoque doctrinis . . . '

I have purposely given this quotation in its Latin form (the authorised English version is given in Appendix I), since any attempt to translate it by a single English sentence inevitably obscures its exact meaning and force to a greater or less extent.

The preceding sentence describes as a very grave danger naturalistic education in the delicate subject of purity of morals. The sentence I have quoted in Latin points out how the danger comes about, and describes in greater detail those educational methods which the preceding sentence had described more sum-marily as 'naturalistic.' The Latin sentence is not couched in the language of a formal prohibition, and in fact does not formally prohibit anything, except of course in so far as that which is 'stupid and dangerous' may be regarded as prohibited. But although there is no formal prohibition, it is perfectly clear that by this sentence a particular procedure or line of conduct is strongly and unequivocally reprobated. That reprobation falls upon 'those, and they are very many, who foolishly and dangerously adopt and promote (or carry into practice) a form of training going by the disagreeable name of sexual education ; such persons who are mistaken enough to suppose that by the use of merely natural means, entirely neglecting the support of religion and piety, they are able to protect the adolescent against unlawful indulgence and excess by subjecting all children, without discrimination of sex and even in public, to instruction and initiation into hazardous and uncertain doctrines.'

A careful examination of this sentence shows us that the fact that instruction is given in public adds yet a further aggravating factor to the other unsatisfactory features which the Pope singles out for explicit mention in the method he reprobates.

But it seems clear that a form of instruction and counsel on sex matters which does *not* rely on merely natural means, which avails itself to the full of the support afforded by religion and piety, and which is not addressed to both sexes indiscriminately, does not fall under this reprobation, even if it takes the form of class instruction, i.e. is given in public. It still remains true however that the public propounding in class of a form of teaching otherwise entirely unexceptionable may be condemnable, although not explicitly on the ground of the extract from the Encyclical quoted above. We now have to consider whether this is the case.

The dangers and disadvantages of class instruction on this subject are at once apparent from what has been said in Chapter VIII. Those difficulties, dangers and disadvantages are truly formidable, and others could easily be added. But the fact that dangers attach to a given procedure does not by that very fact rule that procedure out of court, since even greater dangers may arise from taking no procedure at all. It *may* be that class instruction in certain cases is the only possible alternative to complete inaction in the matter. I don't say that it ever is, and we shall examine this question more carefully presently. But *if* it can be shown that class instruction is the only practical alternative in a given instance to adventuring the children concerned into our modern world unequipped for the experiences they will certainly meet, then we must decide whether class instruction or ignorance carry the greater dangers, and make our choice of the lesser of two evils. After all, even the best parental instruction is obviously not free from danger, and Pope Pius XII recognises this in his Allocution of 25 October, 1941, commending parental instruction, however, because it can be carried out 'with *far less danger* (italics mine) than if they learned them haphazard, from some disturbing encounter, from secret conversations, through information received from over-sophisticated companions, as secrecy inflames the imagination and troubles the senses' ; cf. C.T.S., S.168, p. 12.

Since I have little practical acquaintance with school administration, I am unable to do more than give my opinion, for what it is worth, as to the extent to which in particular instances it may be found impossible to carry out systematic private instruction in school, thus forcing one to face the stark alternative between class instruction and no instruction at all. I have indeed been informed by many teachers in non-Catholic schools, both elementary and county secondary, that the desire to furnish adequate sex instruction has failed to be implemented by reason of the fact that no one on the teaching staff was willing or felt competent to undertake the task. In many such cases recourse has been had to the service of some outside instructor, such as a local medical man or woman, or an accredited lecturer from the Central Council for Health Education. This has, of course, involved class instruction. I feel that if it is decided that instruction in the schools is necessary or desirable, it should be possible in Catholic schools to find teachers willing to undertake private instruction, and that if there is a lack of those *competent* to do so, this defect can be, and should be, speedily remedied. I do not believe therefore that the mediation of sex knowledge to children of school age by the method of collective instruction *alone* is ever peremptorily forced upon us as the only practicable means of meeting the situation.*

I do, however, incline to the view that in many cases *some* form of collective school instruction may be allowable, desirable and even necessary. But it seems clear to me that such collective instruction should always be preceded by private instruction of the individuals concerned, in which those topics can, if necessary, be dealt with which are unsuitable for public discussion. In other words, collective instruction should only be given to those who have already been prepared for it by private instruction. The sort of private instruction I have in mind should be simple, comparatively brief, accurate and extremely clear, adequate without elaboration. Provided such instruction is given to individuals in private, it seems to me that a wide range of more general topics relating to this subject may safely be handled by collective instruction. I confess to being attracted to the view of those who hold that such collective instruction on more general topics relating to sex is most effective when it is, as it were, intermingled in an almost unnoticed manner with other indifferent items of teaching. In the course of normal teaching of such subjects as history, literature, and of course religion, there must surely be abundant opportunities for pointing a lesson about such things as the need for self-control ; effective ways of exercising it ; the dangers and unworthiness of wrong conduct ; the origin, utility and meaning of the proprieties and conventions ; right attitude to and relations with members of the other sex ; the dignity of the married state and the importance

---

* The Joint Pastoral clearly confirms this view, since it expresses strong disapprobation of physiological sex instruction in public as 'fraught with grave dangers' and 'against the traditional teaching of the Church'.

of sound family life ; the moral dangers which the modern attitude to life connotes, etc., all, of course, handled at a time and in a manner adapted to the ages and capacities of the pupils concerned. Some teachers adopt this method very successfully indeed, and it certainly seems far better than devoting specific teaching sessions to the exclusive discussion of topics connected with sex behaviour, however general and delicately handled.* Admittedly this method of 'incidental' teaching *sensim sine sensu* calls for real teaching ability and a good deal of forethought and trouble. And I am not unaware of the fact that the growing tendency towards specialisation of teachers makes it increasingly difficult for a teacher to be in touch with a class

---

* An inspection of the list of topics which it is suggested may be suitably handled by collective instruction should, I think, make it abundantly clear that I am *not* here advocating public sex instruction of children in the sense in which it is commonly understood, and in which it is reprobated in the various documents quoted. Obviously, in the widest possible sense, 'Sex instruction' might be taken to apply to all instruction in which there is any reference to sex, in general or in particular, remote or proximate, direct or indirect. Evidently this cannot be the sense in which 'sex instruction' in public is reprobated, since if this were the case it would prevent any reference in the class-teaching of children to topics connected, however remotely, with sex. Taken quite literally, this would even prevent any reference in class to the sixth or ninth commandments, or to the virtue of purity.

The whole subject has such far-reaching implications in the fields of personal conduct, religion, morality, family relationships, civic duties and responsibilities, social conventions and habits, social structure, social economics, local government, political administration, etc., that it is of great importance that it should be brought into its right relationship with the rest of life in the mind of the child, and thus come to assume its right proportion in the scale of values. It seems to me that this can and must be done in the course of regular class-teaching, preceded by individual instruction from the parent, or his authorised substitute, on the essential physiological facts and their more intimate implications. (If such individual instruction be not provided, the collective instruction on more general topics will, of course, lose much of its efficacy). To audiences of adults and late adolescents it is quite easy to lecture on these general topics connected with sex, without any embarrassment, since there is not the slightest need even to touch on those more intimate considerations which unduly stimulate the imagination and stir the emotions. With classes of children, reference to these more general matters will present greater difficulties, and I feel that the problem of the age at which the child and early adolescent may best be introduced to various aspects of the matter merits earnest consideration and discussion.

I have elsewhere in this book (p. 31) indicated my conviction that there are many important matters affecting sex which cannot possibly be passed on to pre-pubertal children, even by private instruction, and which are yet largely unsuitable for presentation in the collective instruction of adolescents. Some private instruction or guidance of middle and late adolescents will therefore be required in many cases, and it will probably be found that this will normally be furnished at the request of the individual adolescent, provided that, in default of his parents, a reliable and confidential source of information and guidance is made available. It was with this idea in view that Chapter XIV was written.

sufficiently to engage on real education as distinct from mere instruction. But surely the supplanting of educative by merely instructional methods in the schools has had effects which are so evidently disastrous, that the educational reforms towards which we are looking must necessarily embody some reversal, or at least modification, of this tendency to specialisation.

The fact that a distinction is made between what is taught in private and what is taught in class should help to impress on youth that there is a range of topics concerned with this matter, about which suitable public reference is quite reasonable and allowable, in certain circumstances, and another range about which very considerable reticence should be observed. I have already indicated my attitude towards the teaching of biology in the schools (on pages 9–10), and it seems clear that the private instruction I have recommended above should greatly facilitate the teaching of biology in an objective scientific manner with the minimum likelihood of undesirable emotional repercussions.

The Place of Religion in Instruction. Although, as I have indicated with some emphasis on pages 7 and 8, and in Chapter III, religious motives and values must be decisive in this field, I yet believe that a pedagogical mistake may easily be committed by overstressing this aspect of the matter during the actual instruction. Obviously at some point the matter has to be brought into clear and close relationship with the Christian life, religious practices and the means of grace, both in general and in particular, and this is laid down quite unambiguously in the Holy See's instructions discussed on page 6. But it is also important to relate the matter to common sense, and to the natural rational motives for self-control, right order and proper conduct. The precepts of the supernatural order of grace are always built on a solid foundation of natural reasonableness— they lead man, not back against his own nature, but through nature, onward and far beyond. Indeed, it is an important part of sex pedagogy to show that this particular instinct is not basically different from the other urges of human nature, and that the *ordinary* rules for right conduct apply quite exactly to sex-control as well. It is all too easy for youth to get the mistaken idea that sex is so different from everything else that the ordinary rules do not apply—they can thus become *afraid* of it in a wrong and unreasonable sense, and such irrational fear is a prolific source of quite serious trouble in later life. Provided that the religious implications of the matter have once been made perfectly clear, and provided that subsequent instruction is carried out against the general religious background of the Catholic school, it is unwise to mobilise the weightiest religious sanctions to fortify every reference to the subject. It may be necessary and admissible sometimes to invoke the terrors of Hell, the joys of Heaven or the everlasting love manifested on Calvary to counteract the vices of theft or lying, but we habitually recommend such things as honesty and straight dealing for motives connected indeed, but less proximately connected with the Four Last Things. Similarly, provided that the basic religious attitude and vital orientation is what it should be, it is often of great advantage to reduce sex-control to a very ordinary and matter of fact basis. In other words, in our care to avoid Naturalism on the one hand, we must try to avoid the dangers of pietistic obsessionalism and irrational fear on the other. Incidentally, it should be noted that the various instructions of the Holy See lay far more stress on the inspiring and positive aspect of the matter than on the fear-provoking negative aspect—they speak of the 'positive love of purity', and of 'the triumphant purity of innocence', rather than of the havoc and doom of sin. If in our teaching of children we preserve that proportion between glorious promise and dreadful warning which Our Blessed Lord Himself observed in His Gospel utterances, we shall surely be on safe ground ! Above all in this matter of sex, fear is an ill equipment indeed for the sinner who is trying to extricate himself from his fall.

Collective Instruction and the Youth Service. I believe that the collective instruction of older adolescents of the age-range met with in the Youth Service presents somewhat less difficulty than that of school-children. But even in the case of the older adolescents I feel that it would be highly advantageous if such collective instruction as is thought necessary or useful were preceded by short individual interviews. But I am quite certain, as I have already pointed out on pages 31 and 32, that if this subject is opened up at all with adolescents, suitable individual provision must be made for discussing whatever queries they may raise ; *and this certainly cannot be done in public*, nor, even if it were possible, is it desirable that it should be. I believe that a very great social service can be rendered by suitable workers who can so commend themselves to Youth that they will be privileged to be allowed to help them in the problems which the approach to manhood and womanhood brings. I need scarcely say that such guidance is not required with regard to sex matters alone, or even principally, though discussion of some problem connected with sex often leads the youth to open up on his other personal and intimate hopes, fears, projects, plans and ambitions. Not all adults are temperamentally suited for this work, and it is by no means the case that those who are most anxious to engage on it are best suited to do so. Some notion of what such work involves may perhaps be gathered from a perusal of Chapter XIV.

I am convinced that in many cases the last important and vital stages of sex adjustment cannot be brought about otherwise than by private discussion, either with the parent, or, in default of the parent, with a trusted and reliable guide.

XIII

THE PHYSIOLOGICAL FACTS AND METHODS OF TEACHING

I have quite designedly refrained in this book from cataloguing the physiological facts which must evidently appertain to sex instruction. Reliable and well-written accounts of the physiology of sex are already available in pamphlet form. In any case, the necessary facts are few and simple and their suitable presentation has been worked out in several excellent pamphlets which have been scrutinised and modified with great thoroughness by committees of biological and pedagogical experts sitting for that express purpose. Some of these pamphlets are mentioned in the Bibliography. They will be found to be on the whole restrained, economical, and suitably reticent, though at the same time affording an adequate and quite sufficiently complete treatment of the subject. Minor modifications may here and there be advisable, but anyone who has read this book should have no difficulty in making them. The parent or teacher will of course in many cases have to adapt the printed text to an idiom more suitable to the particular pupil or pupils concerned.

Nor have I ventured to indicate in any but the most general way the ages at which the various items of knowledge should be communicated to children. The British Social Hygiene Council and the Central Council for Health Education have drawn up with great care graded courses suitable for the various ages, and these should prove useful guides to parents and teachers.

Still less have I presumed to theorise regarding actual detailed teaching methods to be adopted. My own experiences of teaching young children have been brief and infrequent. I know of no field in which the mere theoriser can make wilder errors than in this. Possibly the appearance of this book may facilitate the production by some skilled and experienced teacher of a suitable training manual for use by parents and those who have to undertake the instruction of children of school age. That such a manual would be warmly welcomed in many quarters I am convinced.

Before leaving this question of the physiological facts apper-
taining to sex knowledge, I feel that I must say a word about
an opinion which I have heard expressed very frequently and
from many quarters, namely that in default of the parents it is
the priest in the confessional who is the proper person to undertake sex instruction. I have never been able to see that this is
either a proper solution or even a practical solution, and I should
have no difficulty in giving a lengthy list of reasons supporting
my view. I am however, absolved from the necessity of any
detailed discussion of this matter by what I take to be a clear
and emphatic prohibition contained in an Instruction of the
Holy Office, dated 17th May, 1943, laying down the principles
to be observed in the confessional with regard to matters affecting
the sixth commandment.

XIV

MISCELLANEOUS HINTS FOR THOSE CALLED UPON TO ADVISE, GUIDE, AND HELP YOUTH IN THIS MATTER

The adult should not give the appearance of feeling that he has
a *right* to the confidence of the adolescent on this topic. Such
confidence must be *freely* given ; it is a great compliment to the
person to whom it is given. It should be regarded as a great
privilege to receive such confidences, and they should be respected
absolutely and inviolably. Nothing contained in such confidences
may be passed on to a third person, except with the express
consent of the person making the confidence. Tender years
do not deprive the individual of the right to keep secret those
matters on which he or she consults *you* and not another. Of
course, it may sometimes be the Counsellor's duty to urge that
certain information should be passed on to parents or other
authorities in the young person's own best interests, but in the
writer's view it is essential that consent to such a course should
first be given, and *freely* given (i.e. not under undue pressure).
Quite apart from the moral obligation of keeping a secret committed to one, if it once transpires that confidence given to a
Counsellor may be passed on to others, all the subsequent
work of that Counsellor will be enormously hindered.

It is scarcely possible to put too great an emphasis on the
fact that the successful training of others demands *self-training*
as a necessary condition. The young are very quick to detect

anything like humbug, and the living example is more powerful than the spoken word. You are unlikely to carry vital conviction to others unless you have first convinced yourself and are living in accordance with those convictions.

Very great *patience* is required by those who wish to be of service to youth in this matter. The writer knows of cases in which an impatient or unsympathetic word has caused the enquirer to shut up like an oyster, and afterwards to endure years of interior misery rather than raise the subject again. It must be clearly realised that it is something of an ordeal for a young person to approach an adult on such a subject. The adolescent is often extraordinarily sensitive. Over and over again young people have sought an interview with the writer, and sat talking of this and that and the other thing, chatting interminably of anything that comes into their minds except the one thing they really wanted to be helped about. And then, in the last two or three minutes, as one is bringing the interview to a close, often as the visitor's hand is on the door-knob to leave, out it comes : 'Oh, there was just one other thing I wanted to ask you about, but I don't quite know how to put it.' Sometimes there may be two or more 'chatty' interviews, and only during the third interview will the sensitive embarrassed soul screw up desperate courage and come to the point.

Sometimes one can expedite the *dénouement*, but this must be done very judiciously—with some cases it is fatal to hurry them. When the *dénouement* comes, it is sometimes a good plan to comment on it straight away in a very matter of fact manner, perhaps saying that the difficulty referred to is one very frequently met with and can be cleared up quite easily. Two or three minutes of this sort of thing gives the enquirer time to simmer down after the great effort that has been made, and the conversation can then be resumed on a two-way basis. Above all, any appearance of being shocked, surprised or amused, must be avoided like the plague.

Often the embarrassed enquirer, seeking for a 'way to put it' will be immensely grateful if the Counsellor 'gets down to tin-tacks' by a simple method of question and answer : 'Does your difficulty concern yourself alone or your relation with someone else ?'—'Is it a question of thought or action ?'—'Is it perhaps something to do with sex ?'—'Yes ?'—'Ah well, then that's probably easily settled ; we all have our difficulties and perplexities in that matter, etc.'

Patience, I say, is required. The adolescent is often an enigma to himself, and we must be very patient in listening to his attempt to explain himself. One can do a tremendous amount of good by being a good and sympathetic listener, and letting it appear that one is genuinely interested and does not grudge the time involved.

Sentimental Attractions. There can be no doubt at all that strong, warm and lasting friendships can spring up between individuals of the same sex, which are entirely healthy and indeed of inestimable value to the persons concerned. A real friendship of this sort involves mutual support ; it should build up and improve both parties to it ; it should also bring advantages to the community at large. History abounds in records of really noble friendships of this kind, and mankind in general has invariably benefited from them. Nothing which is said below should have the effect of discountenancing such sound friendships, or of diminishing the valuable power of making real and lasting friends.

But it not infrequently happens that young people are troubled by the intrusion into their relationship with a companion of the same sex, of a certain quality of emotional tenderness which seems to them of an undesirable nature, and which prompts them to an attitude which does not accord with their reason and their ideals. The dangers of such a situation are obvious, but it is a great mistake to jump to the worst conclusions in every case in which signs of such an attachment are observed. One should be aware, moreover, of the fact that such attachments often give rise to criticism, discussion and scandal-mongering in such a way as to invest the matter with a degree of moral turpitude and debauchery which is certainly non-existent—much misery can be caused by back-biting of this nature, and the wise authority will rely on his own observations, and make his own judgments, rather than accept the reports and interpretations of others at their face value.

Usually it will be found that a young person involved in such an attachment (which of course may be, and often is, quite unsuspected by the individual towards whom the attraction is felt) will be either too soft or too scrupulous in the matter. In the former case, he or she will all too easily indulge in a great deal of emotional phantasy concerned with the object of the attraction—this is damaging and unsettling and *may* eventually lead to actual wrong behaviour. In cases of over-scrupulosity the young man or young woman concerned may conclude progressively (i) that it is wrong to seek the attractive one's company ; (ii) that it is wrong to accept that company if it is offered unsought ; (iii) that they must violently and suddenly break off their existing friendship ; (iv) that they must avoid having to speak to the attractive one ; (v) that they must avoid even the chance of seeing the attractive one ; (vi) that they must not even be in the same room, company or section as the individual for whom they feel an attraction. Such a piling up of subjective moral prohibitions soon threatens to bring life almost to a standstill.

In both cases, either of softness or of scrupulosity, the result is the same—the individual towards whom the attraction is felt occupies far too much of the sufferer's attention, and something very like an obsessional state supervenes. The remedy is to reduce the amount of mental attention devoted to the object of attraction, and if this is achieved the attraction itself will usually dwindle to easily manageable proportions. Suitable 'rules' or advice which Counsellors may give in such cases are : (i) Make up your mind clearly and definitely that in no case and under no circumstances will you allow your attraction to lead you into wrong behaviour of any kind ; (ii) Avoid touching the other person in *any* way which could not be done in the full light of day in public ; (iii) Treat the other person *normally*— seek his company just to the same extent as you seek that of your other friends, and no more ; (iv) Do not markedly avoid him or act in a strange or conspicuous manner with regard to him ; (v) Do not talk or think of the attraction at all. When it recurs to your mind, turn *at once* to some other interesting topic ; (vi) Get a sufficient amount of fresh air and exercise and look after your bodily health. Low health, fatigue and worry often make the imagination very unmanageable and treacherous.

Relationships with the Other Sex. While it is, of course, perfectly normal and healthy that girls and boys of a suitable age should go about together, yet the conclusion is now becoming inescapable that at least some of the conventions and proprieties which have hitherto safeguarded these relationships, must be reinstated. The Counsellor will know best how to do this in accordance with the spirit of the district or class from which those who consult him are drawn. It is obviously difficult, in a publication designed for general use, to do more than mention a few of the relevant topics. It is important that girls should realise that they are largely in control of the situation, and that they have an immense responsibility for the issue of the friendships they contract. If there is true affection, it should operate towards mutual support and mutual self-control—it should give pain to realise that one is the cause of the downfall or the lowering of the ideals of a loved one. A caress or an endearment or a familiarity which a girl thinks little of, *may* have such a violent effect on the boy as to diminish his self-control disastrously. Drink diminishes self-control, and many young people have taken the first, fatal and all too easily repeated step towards immorality when under its influence. In this matter, a girl should be *extremely* conservative when in the company of the

other sex. It might be well to mention some of the circumstances
and contingencies under which it is wrong, imprudent and
improper for a girl and a boy to be alone together. The un-
desirability of receiving presents and notes without the parents'
knowledge might be touched on. A true womanly reserve is
one of the strongest items in a girl's armoury of attractions, and
she lets herself down badly, and almost irreparably if she
abandons it. Let the girl have an almost maternal solicitude
for the well-being of her boy friend, and regard it as her job to
see that no harm comes to him from her association with him—
even from his own fault—she is really the strong one in the
situation. If marriage is in prospect, the memory of an irre-
proachable courtship will be the finest gift each can give to the
other—such a marriage indeed augurs well.

Sublimation. Young people, especially girls perhaps, who are
exhorted to keep their reproductive instinct under control, often
feel that they are being deprived of something essential to a full
rounded-off human life. They feel that, except in the case of
marriage, they are being condemned to half a life. Girls will
sometimes say: 'I don't want to become like Miss So-and-So',
mentioning an inhibited and desiccated spinster of their acquaintance of the rigid, frigid, scarcely human type that is perpetually
being 'shocked,' takes no joy in life, and is chronically censorious
and disapproving. This is a real difficulty and one ought to be
able to meet it. It should be pointed out that the most important
components of the sex instinct, where they do not find issue in
marriage, may find extremely valuable expression on a higher
and more spiritual plane. In text-books of modern psychology
this matter will be found referred to under the heading of
'sublimation'.

The love and loyal devotion through thick and thin which
might have issued in marriage, the protective self-forgetting
solicitude that might have graced actual parenthood, are not
lost, or starved, or discarded and wasted if the way of marriage
is not chosen. They can and should be of immense service in
the world, sweetening, ennobling and giving joy to the lives of
many others. A peculiar strength of soul and a power of furnish-
ing vital support and inspiration attaches to those who, while
remaining unmarried, neither squander the resources of their
personality on immoral indulgence, nor seek to destroy or kill
anything which is radically good in their make-up. It is conscious control in the light of right principles that is to be aimed
at, rather than repression or destruction of a part of one's own
self. The single state need not and should not entail any
'desiccation' or deadening of one's affective sensibilities, rather
it should widen their range and elevate the plane on which they

operate. In nearly every walk of life we find unmarried individuals of the richest personality, whose gifts and services to the community are extremely valuable and even indispensable. It is true that this privilege of giving oneself for the support and enrichment of others on a spiritual plane has to be paid for in the hard cash of a certain unsatisfied longing for some more concrete emotional associations, but it is well worth while. 'He that would find his soul, let him lose it'.

Temperament and Personality in General. Hitherto we have considered the individual almost exclusively from the point of view of the instinctive drive of sex. Evidently there are many other factors that have to be taken into account in guiding and helping the adolescent. But it will be found that sex-orientation will often give the clue to an understanding of the individual's total personality, since social attitude is determined largely by emotional development and this in turn cannot proceed harmoniously unless sex-adjustment is adequate. It is because of its retardation by a failure to secure satisfactory sex-adjustment that we so frequently find a certain infantilism in the emotional life of individuals which makes them emotional misfits in the adult phase which they have now entered. In such cases striking results are sometimes produced by giving the emotionally backward individual some small responsibility, such as that of 'looking after' another boy, or by appointing him to some minor office. Responsibility often precipitates consolidation of character.

Highly favourable results may also be achieved in many cases by convincing the individual of his or her own value and competence in some department of life. Nobody likes to be thought a failure and incompetent. Indeed, the individual will always react to the apprehension of failure, at least on the extra-conscious level. The ill-favoured, incompetent, clumsy and unintelligent child is neglected by most, makes few friends and becomes relegated to the periphery of things. But the human organism *will* have some hold on life and the values which life offers—if not in one way, then in another. Much delinquency, character-deviation, and anti-social behaviour may be understood as a blundering effort on the part of the organism to make *some* sort of entrance into the dynamic aspects of life. *The human being simply will not acquiesce with quiet resignation in total failure* ; and if failure is met with along one path, then another path, and often a deviated one, will be taken. The personality always tries to throw up some kind of compensation for its apprehended inadequacy ; the prudent Counsellor has to ensure that this compensation is on sound and socially useful lines. In the case of delinquent and deficient boys, the teaching of highly-skilled craftsmanship has had the happiest results. In even the most unpromising personalities there is nearly always some feature or interest which can be brought out and developed in such a way as to enhance the individual's conscious adequacy. We must beware of neglecting and squandering the hidden, undeveloped and yet valuable personality-resources of the 'stupid' girl or boy or the social failure.

The Price of Guidance. Those who are privileged to guide youth in the solution of their intimate problems will soon become aware óf the emergence of something like the 'transference situation' of the psychiatrist. In other words, in the measure that they succeed in understanding and helping those whom they advise, they will find a certain affective (or emotional) attachment springing up between them. The dangers of such attachments in the case of a weak-principled Counsellor are obvious and need no further discussion here. Apart from this, the situation has to be accepted and utilised for the purpose of building up the personality of the one who is being guided, keeping an eye always on the desirability of eventually weaning the individual from any strong emotional dependence on oneself. There will, however, always be a certain number of individuals who are unable to do without affective support, and these will tend to have repeated recourse to the Counsellor, as it were for a fresh charge of dynamism and encouragement. This being 'leaned on' by others for habitual support is a somewhat exhausting process and demands great patience, but if it makes it possible for a fellow-creature to maintain a right pathway through life, it is abundantly worth it. One must always be ready to listen and to let people 'blow off steam' at one.

General Health. The Counsellor should aim at acquiring some expert knowledge of the healthy life. Changes in sleep, feeding, exercise, etc., may sometimes be advised. It must be remembered that long-continued nervous or emotional conditions invariably have a considerable effect on the body. As experience widens, the Counsellor may become used to detecting various physical signs which may point to an otherwise unsuspected nervous or anxiety condition. In such cases, moist and clammy palms, for instance, can be noticed when shaking hands. Muscular rigidity and complete spineless flaccidity both tell their tale to the experienced eye. An appearance of anæmia may give a clue regarding the maintaining cause of a difficulty about which one is consulted. Complaints of palpitation, of feeling 'as if the stomach is turning over,' or of muscular strain and stiffness at the back of the neck, all serve to fill in the total picture to the experienced interviewer. Such matters cannot be adequately dealt with here, and are only mentioned by way of reminding

Counsellors that nothing which affects the human organism is alien to their field. Exact and competent knowledge is required—a little knowledge is a dangerous thing if one is not aware of one's own limitations. All that one may reasonably hope, is to be able to recognise some of the conditions which call for medical intervention. 'Mens sana in corpore sano'.

Expert Psychological Help. The Counsellor will probably come across quite a large number of cases in which specialist psychological advice or treatment is required. For this reason, it will be of great advantage to keep in touch with the local Child Guidance Clinic, or with a medical man or woman with psychological qualifications and experience. It has been the writer's experience that the personnel of Child Guidance Clinics and similar institutions are most ready and willing to help and co-operate in Youth Work.

It is true that many of the anomalies and instabilities of adolescence which used to be looked upon as presaging a pathological future are now found to dissipate entirely in the course of development. But the psychiatrist is so busy nowadays that he is not usually to be found looking for more work, and is unlikely therefore to assess every vagary of youth as a pathological manifestation. At the same time it must be remembered that most of the psychic disorders from which adults suffer had their beginnings in early youth, and in very many cases could have been remedied, had they been tackled in their early stages.

Moreover, it is a mistake to regard the psychiatrist, or indeed the medical man in general, as concerned exclusively with the negative task of preventing and remedying morbid conditions. Medicine, and particularly psychological medicine, has a more positive social function in seeking to create and maintain conditions under which the best and noblest values of life can emerge to an extent of which we have scarcely yet dreamed. This business of Youth Guidance demands the best we can give it, and the most expert advice we can obtain regarding it.

Motives and Morale. It is the writer's emphatic opinion that in our dealings with Youth we must constantly offer the best, the highest, the most noble motives and ideals. We have no right to offer anything less, and our first job as Youth Leaders is to ensure that our own personalities are fit channels for the mediation of such elevated motives. In the adolescent we have the fresh heart of a new man leaping up to its arduous, glorious, manful destiny. We must give the adolescent reality, and not that watered-down version of it which represents our own jaded compromise with life. There are those who maintain that Youth will not respond to the really big ideals—they are wrong ; this is an error and a poisonous error.

Whatever our views may be as to war aims in detail, we are surely agreed that we are fighting for the survival of the things that are good and just and right. When victory in the field has been secured, we shall be faced with an even more arduous task of building a world in which the good and the right can be maintained and enhanced. That, and no less, is the terrific fateful task which awaits our Youth, and we must strain every nerve and give of our best to equip them for it. Youth wants big thoughts and big motives to get its teeth into—woe betide us if we fail to supply them !

We still lack an all-embracing affective drive behind our war effort, mighty enough to match up even approximately to the terrific emotional drive behind the Germans and the Japanese. Fear and hate propaganda will not supply it for us. The sands are running out, and the morale of the nation still lags sadly behind the dignity and sublimity of the task destiny has laid upon us. If we fulfil our obligations to Youth adequately, our own morale will rise to the situation, and we shall ensure that the end of the war will find our Youth 'on its toes', ready for the finest hour in the chequered history of mankind.

APPENDIX I

EXTRACTS FROM ROMAN DOCUMENTS DEALING WITH THIS QUESTION

(1) **The Rescript of the Congregation of the Index to the Bishop of Barcelona,** 18 January, 1908. The Bishop's enquiry concerned the books 'Lo que debe saber el nino' ('What the boy ought to know') and 'Lo que debe saber la nina' ('What the girl ought to know'), both of them translations from English originals. In the reply, the Congregation said : ' . . . it is in no way fitting that adolescents in Spain should be instructed and taught according to the rules laid down in the books mentioned ; but it is necessary that the books concerned should be withdrawn from the possession of the faithful, and especially from adolescents.'

(2) **The Rescript of the Congregation of the Holy Office,** 21 March, 1931. The question proposed to the Congregation was: Can that way of procedure be approved which is called 'sexual education' or even 'sexual initiation' ? The Congregation's answer was as follows : 'The reply to the question is in the negative ; in the education of youth that method is to be faithfully retained which has been used hitherto by the Church and the Saints, and which is commended by His Holiness the Pope

in his Encyclical on 'The Christian Education of Youth' of 31/12/29. Accordingly special care is to be paid to the complete, solid and continuous religious instruction of the youth of both sexes ; awakening in them a high regard and desire for, and a love of, the angelical virtue ; teaching them as a matter of supreme importance to be persevering in prayer, to make assiduous use of the Sacraments of Penance and the Holy Eucharist, to honour the holy purity of the Blessed Virgin Mother with filial devotion, and to commit themselves unreservedly to her protection, teaching them moreover carefully to avoid dangerous reading, indecent scenic performances, wrong conversations and all other occasions of sin. Consequently works which have recently been written and published, even by certain Catholic authors, advocating a new method of procedure, are in no wise to be approved.'

(3) **The Encyclical of Pope Pius XI** *Divini Illius Magistri* (On the Christian Education of Youth), 31 December, 1929. 'The family therefore holds directly from the Creator the mission and hence the right to educate the offspring, a right inalienable because inseparably joined to the strict obligation, a right anterior to any right whatever of civil society and of the State, and therefore inviolable on the part of any power on earth. . . .'

The wisdom of the Church in this matter is expressed with precision and clearness in the Code of Canon Law, can. 1113 : 'Parents are under a grave obligation to see to the religious and moral education of their children, as well as to their physical and civic training, as far as they can, and moreover to provide for their temporal well-being . . .'

In fact it must never be forgotten that the subject of Christian education is man whole and entire, soul united to body in unity of nature, with all his faculties natural and supernatural, such as right reason and revelation show him to be ; man, therefore, fallen from his original estate, but redeemed by Christ and restored to the supernatural condition of adopted son of God, though without the preternatural privileges of bodily immortality or perfect control of appetite. There remain therefore in human nature the effects of original sin, the chief of which are weakness of will and disorderly inclinations . . .

Hence every form of pedagogic naturalism which in any way excludes or weakens supernatural Christian formation in the teaching of youth, is false . . .

Another very grave danger is that naturalism which nowadays invades the field of education in that most delicate matter of purity of morals. Far too common is the error of those who with dangerous assurance and under an ugly term propagate a so-called sex-education, falsely imagining they can forearm youths against the dangers of sensuality by means purely natural, such as a foolhardy initiation and precautionary instruction for all indiscriminately, even in public ; and worse still, by exposing them at an early age to the occasions, in order to accustom them, so it is argued, and as it were to harden them against such dangers.

Such persons grievously err in refusing to recognise the inborn weakness of human nature, and the law of which the Apostle speaks, fighting against the law of the mind, and also in ignoring the experience of facts, from which it is clear that, particularly in young people, evil practices are the effect not so much of ignorance of intellect as of weakness of a will exposed to dangerous occasions, and unsupported by the means of grace.

In this extremely delicate matter, if, all things considered, some private instruction is found necessary and opportune, from those who hold from God the commission to teach and who have the grace of state, every precaution must be taken.'

(4) **The Encyclical of Pope Pius XI** *Casti Connubii* (on Christian Marriage) 31 December, 1930. 'And there can be no doubt that, by natural and divine law, the right and duty of educating offspring belong primarily to those who, having begun the work of nature by begetting children, are absolutely forbidden to leave unfinished the work they have begun and so expose it to inevitable ruin.

. . . It is of the first importance that the faithful should be well instructed concerning marriage ; instructed by the spoken and by the written word, not once or superficially but frequently and thoroughly, and with clear and weighty arguments, so that these truths may take hold of their minds and move their hearts.

. . . This salutary teaching, this religious science of matrimony, bears no resemblance to that exaggerated physiological education which the so-called reformers of our day offer as a beneficent service to married folk. They dilate much on these questions of physiology ; but what they teach by it is more the art of skilful sinning than the virtue of chaste living.

. . . All this . . . depends in great measure upon the suitable preparation, remote as well as proximate, of the parties for marriage. Indeed it can hardly be denied that the firm foundation of a happy marriage and the ruin of an unhappy one have been prepared already in the souls of men and women during the days of their childhood and youth. Those who before marriage were in all things self-seeking and indulged their passions, will, it is to be feared, be the same in marriage as they were before it ; they will reap what they have sown, and in their home will reign unhappiness, mutual disdain, misunderstandings, and boredom with each other's company . . . worst of all, they may even find themselves with their passions still untamed.

Let young men and women, therefore, approach wedlock well disposed and well prepared, so that they may be able to help one another to face the adversities of life side by side, and, what is far more important, attain their eternal salvation and shape their interior life according to the age of the fulness of Christ. This will also enable them to be the more easily to their children parents such as God wants them to be to their little ones : a father who is truly a father, a mother who is truly a mother ; parents whose loving care will cause their children, even in spite of great poverty and amidst this vale of tears, to find in their home some likeness to that happy Paradise of delights in which the Creator of the human race placed its first members. In this way, too, they will make their children perfect men and perfect Christians, inspiring them with a truly Catholic spirit and training them to that noble love of country which piety and gratitude requires of us.

Therefore those who intend at some time to enter the holy state of matrimony, as well as those who are concerned with the education of Christian youth, will attach great importance to these counsels, thus preparing the way for blessings and forestalling evils. They will also bear in mind the warning which We gave in Our Encyclical on Education : ''From childhood, inclinations which are evil must be repressed and inclinations which are good must be fostered and encouraged. The minds of children must above all be imbued with the doctrines which come from God, and their hearts strengthened with the assistance of divine grace. Without these none will be able to master his own desires, nor will it be possible to expect the full and perfect results of the teaching and training of the Church, whom God has provided with heavenly doctrines and with divine Sacraments precisely in order that she may be the effective Teacher of all mankind''.'

(5) **The Papal Allocution of Pius XII,** 26 October, 1941. 'We are mindful of the immortal Pope Pius XI, who treated so profoundly of the Christian education of the young. Dealing with this subject . . . he then went on regretfully to observe that parents are often unprepared or ill-equipped for their work as educators. Accordingly, and since the limits of that lucid and exhaustive document did not permit him to deal in detail with education in the home, he exhorted in the name of Christ all pastors of souls ''to use every means, by catechism and instruction, by word of mouth and in widely published writings, to ensure that Christian parents are well instructed both in general and in particular regarding their duties in the religious, moral and civic education of their children, and regarding the best

methods . . . apart from their own example . . . of attaining that end.''

. . . Many of the moral characteristics which you see in the youth or the man owe their origin to the manner and circumstances of his first upbringing in infancy : purely organic habits contracted at that time may later prove a serious obstacle to the spiritual life of the soul. And so you will make it your special care in the treatment of your child to observe the prescriptions of a perfect hygiene, so that when it comes to the use of reason its bodily organs and faculties will be healthy and robust and free from distorted tendencies.

. . . From that early age a loving look, a warning word, must teach the child not to yield to all its impressions, and as reason dawns it must learn to discriminate and to master the vagaries of its sensations ; in a word, under the guidance and admonition of the mother it must begin the work of its own education.

Study the child in his tender age. If you know him well you will educate him well ; you will not misconceive his character ; you will come to understand him, knowing when to give way and when to be firm ; a naturally good disposition does not fall to the lot of all the sons of men.

Train the mind of your children. Do not give them wrong ideas or wrong reasons for things ; whatever their questions may be, do not answer them with evasions or untrue statements which their minds rarely accept, but take occasion from them lovingly and patiently to train their minds, which want only to open to the truth and to grasp it with the first ingenuous gropings of their reasoning and reflective powers . . .

. . . But the day will come when the childish heart will feel new impulses stirring within it ; new desires will disturb the serenity of those early years. In that time of trial, Christian mothers, remember that to train the heart means to train the will to resist the attacks of evil and the insidious temptations of passion ; during that period of transition from the unconscious purity of infancy to the triumphant purity of adolescence you have a task of the highest importance to fulfil. You have to prepare your sons and daughters so that they may pass with unfaltering step, like those who pick their way among serpents, through that time of crisis and physical change ; and pass through it without losing anything of the joy of innocence, preserving intact that natural instinct of modesty with which Providence has girt them as a check upon wayward passions. That sense of modesty, which in its spontaneous abhorrence from the impure is akin to the sense of religion, is made of little account in these days ; but you, mothers, will take care that they do not lose it through indecency in dress or self-adornment, through unbecoming familiarities or immoral spectacles ; on the contrary you will seek to make it more delicate and alert, more upright and sincere. You will keep a watchful eye on their steps ; you will not suffer the whiteness of their souls to be stained and contaminated by corrupt and corrupting company ; you will inspire them with a high esteem and jealous love for purity, advising them to commend themselves to the sure and motherly protection of the Immaculate Virgin. Finally, with the discretion of a mother and a teacher, and thanks to the open-hearted confidence with which you have been able to inspire your children, you will not fail to watch for and to discern the moment in which certain unspoken questions have occurred to their minds and are troubling their senses. It will then be your duty to your daughters, the father's duty to your sons, carefully and delicately to unveil the truth as far as it appears necessary, to give a prudent, true, and Christian answer to those questions, and set their minds at rest. If imparted by the lips of Christian parents, at the proper time, in the proper measure, and with the proper precautions, the revelation of the mysterious and marvellous laws of life will be received by them with reverence and gratitude, and will enlighten their minds with far less danger than if they learned them haphazard, from some disturbing encounter, from secret conversations, through information received from over-sophisticated companions, or from clandestine reading, the more dangerous and pernicious as secrecy inflames the imagination and troubles the senses . . . '

APPENDIX II

THE JOINT PASTORAL

Since this book was written and revised for the Press, there has been published a Joint Pastoral Letter of the Hierarchy of England and Wales on the Catholic Attitude to Sex Education. In view of the great importance and permanent usefulness of this document, we reproduce it here in full ; the only changes being the use of small print for quotations from Roman documents already quoted *in extenso* elsewhere in this book.

THE ARCHBISHOPS AND BISHOPS OF ENGLAND AND WALES TO THE CLERGY AND FAITHFUL OF THE SAID COUNTRIES HEALTH AND BENEDICTION IN THE LORD.

DEARLY BELOVED BRETHREN AND
DEAR CHILDREN IN JESUS CHRIST :

The publication of the Board of Education's pamphlet on sex education in schools and youth organizations* has brought

---

* H.M. Stationery Office, 1943.

the subject into prominence and calls for some statement concerning the Catholic attitude towards the problem.

We have no desire to minimize the necessity of some attention being paid to the problem both now and continuously in the future. But the remedy is to be found not so much in the imparting in public of fuller and more systematic knowledge of sex from the physiological or biological standpoint as by the removal of external temptations and by the general and determined inculcation of the practice of Christian virtue and our dependence on divine grace.

'Far too common,' said Pope Pius XI, 'is the error of those who, with dangerous assurance and under an ugly term, propagate a so-called sex education, falsely imagining they can forearm youths against the dangers of sensuality by means purely natural, such as a foolhardy initiation and precautionary instruction for all indiscriminately, even in public ; and worse still, exposing them, at an early age, to the occasions in order to accustom them, so it is argued, and as it were to harden them against such dangers. Such persons,'' says the Pope, 'grievously err in refusing to recognize the inborn weakness of human nature and the law of which the Apostle speaks, fighting against the law of the mind ;* and also in ignoring the experience of facts, from which it is clear that, particularly in young people, evil practices are the effect not so much of ignorance of intellect as of weakness of a will exposed to dangerous occasions and unsupported by the means of grace.'†

If the problem with which we are concerned is accentuated in these days it is due, apart from wartime conditions, (1) to certain general influences which are responsible for placing before young people lower moral standards of life and conduct, and (2) to the failure on the part of many parents to fulfil the obligation which is theirs of instructing their children in the things which concern the welfare of body and soul. The proposed instruction in the schools would be largely unnecessary if the causes of the evils which it is intended to remedy were, first of all, removed—bad literature, bad pictures, bad theatre displays, shocking housing conditions. It is our opinion that these evils can and should be removed. As regards the parental instruction of children in the matters concerned, we are convinced that herein lies the chief cause and the remedy which is being sought. There is to-day a lamentable decline in family education due largely to an ever-increasing tendency on the part of parents deliberately to shirk their obvious duty. Parents should remember that the obligation to see to the religious and moral education of their children rests primarily on themselves and that there are certain aspects of this education which cannot satisfactorily be delegated to others.‡ 'However eminent school-teachers may be in their profession,' said Pope Pius XII, addressing Catholic

---

* Rom. vii. 23. † Encyclical *Divini illius magistri*, 31 Dec., 1929.

‡ Cf. Code of Canon Law, Cn. 1113.

mothers, 'they will have little success in the formation of your children without your collaboration.'* 'To women, more than to anyone else,' continued the Pope, 'is entrusted the first education of the child in its early months and years.'† The omission of parental instruction and parental discipline is undoubtedly responsible for many of the moral and social evils which we regret to-day. At the same time we are aware that even good parents sometimes feel themselves unprepared or ill equipped for their work as educators, not only with regard to subjects which are now universally taught by specially trained teachers in the schools, but also with regard to matters which have, so far, been considered of a more intimate and personal nature and, accordingly, are more properly the sphere of the home. The Catholic Church does not encourage such unpreparedness on the part of parents, nor does she, as some have thought, favour a policy of complete secrecy between parents and children concerning the mysteries of life. Any doubts upon this have been set at rest by the pronouncements of recent Popes. 'Train the mind of your children,' said the present Holy Father to the gathering of Catholic mothers on the Feast of Christ the King, 1941 ; 'do not give them wrong ideas or wrong reasons for things ; whatever their questions may be, do not answer them with evasions or untrue statements which their minds rarely accept, but take occasion from them lovingly and paternally to train their minds, which want only to open to the truth and to grasp it with the first ingenuous gropings of their reasoning and reflective powers.' Catholic parents can depend on the grace of the sacrament of matrimony and upon the additional help which comes from prayer and the frequent reception of the sacraments of Penance and the Holy Eucharist to carry out this advice of the head of the Church with the desired results. Those seeking suggestions as to how the counsels of the Pope can be carried out with more full effect will find help in an increasing number of publications from reliable Catholic sources.

Nevertheless in treating of these delicate matters 'every precaution must be taken' even by parents.‡ 'Such is our misery and inclination to sin,' says a well-known Christian writer quoted by Pope Pius XI, 'that often in the very things considered to be remedies against sin, we find occasions for and inducements to sin itself. Hence it is of the highest importance that a good father, while discussing with his son a matter so delicate, should be well on his guard and not descend to details, nor refer to the

---

* Alloc., 26 Nov., 1941.

† *Ibid.*

‡ Cf. Pius XI, *Divini illius magistri.*

various ways in which this deadly hydra destroys with its poison so large a portion of the world ; otherwise it may happen that, instead of extinguishing this fire, he unwittingly stirs or kindles it in the simple and tender heart of the child. Speaking generally,' concludes the same writer, 'during the period of childhood it suffices to employ those remedies which produce the double effect of opening the door to the virtue of purity and closing the door upon vice.'*

Unfortunately, until parents are better equipped for their task, and do in fact carry out their obligations, there will always be some children lacking in the knowledge of those things intended by God for their own progress in virtue and for the fulfilment of God's designs. But we do not admit that, therefore, the duty of imparting this knowledge necessarily falls upon the school-teachers. Teachers have no strict right to arrogate to themselves parental duties ; if called upon by the parents to deputize for them in this delicate matter they may very properly do so. Whilst we willingly and readily pay tribute to the high-mindedness of the majority of the school-teachers of this country, and whilst we acknowledge with deep appreciation their contribution towards the welfare of our children and the common good, we feel it necessary to insist that the teacher is primarily 'in place of the parent' (*in loco parentis*) and not a civil servant doing the work of the State. Accordingly, a teacher must always respect the rights and wishes of the parents concerning the education of children, and rather than taking over parental duties should regard it as their task to help parents towards the proper fulfilment of obligations.

This is not to belittle or depreciate the help which individual teachers have, in their charity, given to individual children concerning even the more intimate matters of life. There will, unfortunately, always be some parents who neglect their obvious duties towards their children and whose omissions call for attention by someone else. In such cases the teacher or experienced youth-leader, animated by Christian charity and having the necessary competence, may be the best person to make up the deficiency. But it is advisable that the approval of the parents should always be sought. This help, however, on the more intimate matters of life must always remain personal and individual. Class or group instruction of children or of youth on the physiological aspect of sex would be fraught with grave dangers and would be against the traditional teaching of the Church.

To the question whether the method called 'sexual education' or even 'sexual initiation' could be approved, the Supreme

---

* Silvio Antoniano, *Dell'educazione cristiana dei figliuoli*, lib. II, c88, *ibid.*

Sacred Congregation of the Holy Office, on 21st March, 1931, replied 'in the negative', and directed that 'the method of educating youth employed by the Church and holy men in the past, and commended by Pope Pius XI in the encyclical on "The Christian Education of Youth", 31st December, 1929, must be preserved.' The method commended by the Pope, in the encyclical referred to, is clear. 'In this extremely delicate matter,' says the Holy Father, 'if, all things considered, some individual instruction is found necessary and opportune from those who hold from God the commission to educate and who have the grace of state, every precaution must be taken. Such precautions are well known in traditional Christian education.' These words, taken in conjunction with the decree of the Holy Office, leave no room to doubt that the Church is opposed to collective or public sex education with or without supposed 'safeguards'. She teaches that, in place of such methods of sex education,

'care must be taken, in the first place, to give a full, firm, and uninterrupted religious instruction to youth of both sexes ; that an esteem and desire for and love of the angelic virtue be instilled into them ; that they shall be urged, especially to be instant in prayer, assiduous in the reception of the sacraments of Penance and the Holy Eucharist ; that they shall cultivate a filial devotion to the Blessed Virgin, Mother of holy purity, and place themselves under her protection ; and that they shall carefully avoid danger-ous reading, immodest shows, bad company, and all occasions of sin.'*

This attitude of the Church is not obscurantist, as some may suggest, but is based on her two thousand years' experience and upon her unrivalled knowledge of human nature. Moreover, it is an attitude which is supported by eminent educationists and psychologists. The late Professor Münsterberg, the noted American psychologist and, incidentally, a non-Catholic, in his famous essay on 'Sex Education', wrote : 'It is hardly possible to disagree on the one factor of the situation, the existence of horrid calamities, and of deplorable abuses in the world of sex. To recognise these abscesses in the social organism necessarily means for every decent being the sincere and enthusiastic hope of removing them. There cannot be any dissent. . . . But while there must be perfect agreement about the moral duty of the social community, there can be the widest disagreement about the right method of carrying on this fight. The popular view of the day is distinctly that, as these evils were hidden from sight by the policy of silence, the right method of removing them from the world must be the opposite scheme, the policy of unveiled speech. The overwhelming majority has come to this conclusion as if it were a matter of course. The man in the street and, what is more surprising, the woman in the home are convinced that

---

* Decree of the Holy Office, 21 March, 1931.

E

if we disapprove of those evils we must first of all condemn the silence of our forefathers. They feel as if he who sticks to the belief in silence must necessarily help the enemies of society, and become responsible for the alarming increase of sexual affliction and crime. They refuse to see that on the one side the existing facts and the burning need for their removal, and on the other side the question of the best method and best plan for the fight, are entirely distinct, and that the highest intention for social reform may go together with the deepest conviction that the popular method of the present day is doing incalculable harm, is utterly wrong, and is one of the most dangerous causes of that evil which it hopes to destroy.'*

The reason for the recent agitation in certain quarters for more general sex instruction is not altogether clear to us. If its main purpose is a social one, namely, to safeguard the physical welfare of the nation, then the advocates of sex instruction on the lines suggested are doomed to disappointment, since the evils concerned are the effect not so much of ignorance as of a weakness of will unsupported by the means of grace. Information alone will not produce a healthy and sound nation ; much less will it be sufficient to prepare souls for their eternal destiny in the next life. It is not so much information as *formation* which is required—formation of character, the training of the mind, the heart, and the will with the necessary assistance of religion. The religious and moral training must continue to be the main method of approach in the schools and youth movements to the problems we are seeking to solve. The psychological aspect will doubtless have increasingly interesting contributions to offer, but the supernatural Christian formation must always provide the foundation of the ideal education of youth. Every other form of education is false and unsound and will lead neither to spiritual nor temporal well-being. We exhort our Catholic teachers and youth leaders, therefore, to continue in their holy vocation and to be instant in helping to form those in their charge in the ways of Christian virtue. We regard our Catholic schools as sanctuaries wherein our children are mightily strengthened in the faith and its practice. Nevertheless, the school or the youth centre must always remain complementary to the home and must not supplant it. Even if parents are found to be neglecting duties which are essentially parental and which cannot be normally undertaken as satisfactorily by others, the State should hesitate, by teaching in the schools or by other means, to encourage parents in their neglect. The State should rather take steps to see that parents themselves are better equipped for their parental tasks.

---

* Cf. *Psychology and Social Sanity*, by Hugo Münsterberg.

This encouragement of the fulfilment of parental responsibility will, indeed, be the first endeavour of the Church. With this in view we endorse the appeal of Pius XI to all pastors of souls 'to use every means, by catechisms and instruction, by word of mouth and in widely published writings, to ensure that Christian parents are well instructed both in general and in particular regarding their duties in the religious, moral, and civic education of their children, and regarding the best methods—apart form their own example—of attaining that end.'* In carrying out this commission the clergy will, no doubt, find helpful those gatherings, organizations, and confraternities of Catholic parents, mothers, and adolescents which the Holy Father refers to as 'worthy of all praise and encouragement.'†

We appeal to all Catholic parents to respond to the general effort which will be made on their behalf and to co-operate wholeheartedly in trying to equip themselves adequately for their noble task. We feel sure that with generous co-operation on the part of parents we shall not only go far to remove the present grave social and moral evils but that we shall help to build up a generation whose delight it will be to 'seek the things that are above' and whose purity and integrity of life will be a joy both to God and man.

Given at Westminster on the Feast of St. Anselm in the year of Our Lord nineteen hundred and forty-four, and appointed to be read in all the churches and chapels of England and Wales on the third Sunday after Easter.

✠ BERNARD, *Archbishop of Westminster.*
✠ RICHARD, *Archbishop of Liverpool.*
✠ THOMAS, *Archbishop of Birmingham.*
✠ MICHAEL, *Archbishop of Cardiff.*
✠ PETER, *Archbishop-Bishop of Southwark.*
✠ ARTHUR, *Bishop of Brentwood.*
✠ THOMAS, *Bishop of Middlesbrough.*
✠ JOHN, *Bishop of Plymouth.*
✠ WILLIAM, *Bishop of Clifton.*
✠ AMBROSE, *Bishop of Shrewsbury.*
✠ HENRY JOHN, *Bishop of Leeds.*
✠ JOSEPH, *Bishop of Hexham and Newcastle.*
✠ THOMAS EDWARD, *Bishop of Lancaster.*
✠ HENRY VINCENT, *Bishop of Salford.*
✠ LEO, *Bishop of Northampton.*
✠ DANIEL, *Bishop of Menevia.*
✠ JOHN HENRY, *Bishop of Portsmouth.*
✠ EDWARD, *Bishop-Elect of Nottingham.*

---

* *Divini illius magistri.*   † *Ibid.*

APPENDIX III

MEMORANDUM ON SEX EDUCATION
Published with the approval of the Bishops of Scotland

The importance of this question prompts us to submit a memorandum on it.

We view all talk of sex-instruction and sex-teaching with instinctive distrust. Many people say today that some sort of sex-instruction is necessary because youth is becoming less amenable to good influence and more attracted to dangerous pleasures. We sympathise with their viewpoint. Like them we are alarmed at the fact that young people read books without scruple and see plays and films without shame which are not only coarse and vulgar but often grossly immoral. At the same time we are perturbed at the suggestions put forward by well-intentioned reformers and are of the firm opinion that the remedy of sex-instruction, so strongly advocated in many quarters, instead of curing the evil will greatly aggravate it. We therefore feel it our duty to draw attention to the perils involved, and to indicate what we think to be the solution to this most difficult question.

At the outset we should like to stress that Catholic tradition and policy is not one of complete silence and concealment. In this matter ignorance is not necessarily bliss. Few youths today are blissfully ignorant ; the tragedy is that their knowledge often comes from a tainted source. What they are ignorant of is the sacredness of sex and its proper place in the life of the individual and of society. But whilst our tradition is not one of silence it is nevertheless based on well defined principles and on a clear matrimonial doctrine and practice. It is from this point that we would begin.

As a basic principle we hold strongly to the view that the health of society is dependent on the permanent stability of marriage and on a good home life. The home is nature's training ground for good living, and, as we stressed in a previous memorandum, for learning and practising those virtues which make for good citizenship. Educational measures which touch upon the family should therefore be expressly designed to assist the family to fulfil its function. They should in no way delegate to other institutions duties which by nature belong to the family. Any infringement of this basic principle we believe is bound to be to the detriment of society.

Following from this arise secondary though no less important principles.

(1) It must be accepted by all as part of our moral code that in marriage sexual pleasure is good, lawful, in fact holy ; but that outside marriage it is sinful, irrational and animal. This principle should be clearly taught to all adolescents.

(2) The bond established by nature between parent and child is so close that such an intimate and sacred subject as discussion of sex is primarily a matter for parent and child.

(3) The proper approach to the whole question of sex and marriage is the moral and spiritual approach.

(4) Full recognition must therefore be given to the inborn weakness of human nature, and to the consequent fact that ' evil practices are the effect not so much of ignorance as of weakness of a will exposed to dangerous occasion.' (Pius XI).

Coupling these principles with the proposal so much advocated of giving sex-instruction to young people we are led to make these observations.

(1) Without due safeguards factual instruction in sex anatomy is wholly wrong in principle. The sexual instinct is inherent in human nature. It will assert itself without ' initiation.' That is why it is called an ' instinct.' Moreover it is one of the strongest of our instincts, which, if not properly controlled and channelled can cause havoc in society. Immeasurably more important than any imparting of factual information is the training of the will and the formation of moral character. We cannot stress enough that no amount of *mere knowledge* of sexual functions will train the young to resist the imperious instincts of human nature until they can be lawfully exercised in the marriage state. Positive *training in purity* should be the dominant note, rather than mere factual instruction in sex anatomy, which seems to be what most people mean when they talk of ' sex-initiation.'

(2) We are violently opposed to mass sex-instruction being given publicly and indiscriminately. Experience has shown, with all due respect to witnesses who support the opposite point of view, that mass sex-instruction instead of being a remedy for sin becomes an occasion of it. It opens the door not to the virtue of purity but to vice.

Our firm conviction of the dangers attached to such mass instruction is based on the following reasons :—

(*a*) The sex instinct awakens in different children at different ages. To bring such matters to the notice of an innocent child because it happens to be one of a class and because the subject of the day happens to be sex, is to produce a severe shock in that young mind and is a gross injustice.

(*b*) The instinct is sufficiently strong in human nature without having it discussed in public. The latter course will result in subsequent, and often dangerous, discussion amongst the children themselves.

(c) Contrary to what so-called educationalists may say, it offends the inborn delicacy of children, most especially innocent children, to hear sex matters explained in public. Thus the Catholic attitude in this matter is not stubborn conservatism but common sense, essential for a healthy mentality in the nation.

(d) Sex is such a delicate matter, as psychologists readily attest, that any information which has to be given should be imparted privately, discreetly and personally in a perfectly natural manner by a parent or some lawfully delegated substitute.

(e) The history of the world has not yet furnished proof of any need of detailed lessons in sexual physiology. It has, however, given repeated proof of the need both of forearming youth against the dangers of sensuality and of emphasising self-control and purity of life. Knowledge of the immediate physical aspect of sex behaviour is widespread, but the confusion of mind, and ignorance, regarding the true functions of sex in life is almost equally great. This is very patent when discredit and shame are attached to persons because of certain results following from immoral conduct, while the conduct itself escapes condemnation.

(f) To be fair, any sex information, if necessary at all, must be adapted to the age, temperament, and knowledge of the child. If this personal approach is found essential in the unemotional matter of vocational guidance, surely it is even more vital in a highly emotional matter which goes to the very root of the soul and character.

We said that we did not advocate a policy of complete silence, nor did we consider that children should be left to pick up their knowledge from outside, possibly tainted, sources. If a youth is to be trained in the virtue of purity, some minimum knowledge of the facts of life is necessary. We now suggest, therefore, how we think this knowledge can be best communicated.

Town life, which is the life of the majority of our youth, prevents children from observing the habits of other living beings. Thus they are at a disadvantage compared with children who are country-bred. The simplest and best way to acquire the essential elementary facts is from a parent in a good normal home. We suggest as examples two occasions.

(a) When there is an addition to the family the other children will want to know where it comes from. Instead of telling them lies or evading their questions the parents should tell them enough of the origin of life to allay their natural curiosity. This knowledge should be proportioned to their years.

(b) When it is seen that a child is beginning to be disturbed by sexual thoughts and imaginations (and the parent is in the closest contact and in a position to observe this) the child should be made to understand that these desires are connected with the birth of children and are good and lawful for married people. Some children deduce this for themselves ; others do not, and these latter should be told as part of their training in purity.

The natural person to give this information is the parent. The fact that so many shirk this duty is all the more reason why we should insist on parents realising their responsibility in this important matter. We are not of course averse to other responsible persons giving this information at the request or with the consent of the parents, but it must be given individually and should comprise a minimum of factual knowledge. Its sole purpose should be to assist the formation of the virtue of chastity.

There are two points we would make in conclusion :

(1) As we said in a previous memorandum, and as we are pleased to note the Advisory Council state in their memorandum on citizenship, religion must be the basis of true education. Since training of the will is vital in the matter of sex, the importance of religion in this regard speaks for itself. It is therefore essential that the whole question of sex should be given its proper place in the Christian philosophy of life. As it has been recently put, if children will not be virtuous for the love of God they will not be virtuous at the behest of an education authority.

(2) The sex impulse is easily stimulated, and if frequently or repeatedly stimulated in young people may become well nigh uncontrollable. In view of this and in fairness to the coming generation, to the educational system as a whole and to the moral fibre of the nation, we lay the greatest emphasis on the crying need of a strict control of all literature, films and plays with which youth comes into contact. The best of character training by the best of teachers can be undone by unbecoming literature and films.

PUBLICATIONS WHICH MAY BE CONSULTED

Papal Encyclical ; 'On the Christian Education of Youth'. Catholic Truth Society, No. S.99.

Papal Encyclical ; 'Christian Marriage'. C.T.S., No. DO.113.

Papal Allocution ; 'The Pope speaks to Mothers'. C.T.S. No. S.168.

ANON ; 'Courtship for Girls and Practical Instruction for those about to be Married'. C.T.S., No. S.129.

ANON ; 'Preparing our Daughters for Life' (for Adults), by a Catholic Mother. C.T.S., No. S.165.

BRUCKNER, S.J., P. J. ; 'Sex Instructions. A Guide for Parents, Teachers and Others responsible for the Training of Young People'. The Queen's Work, 3742 West Pine Boulevard, St. Louis, Mo. ; 25 cents, pp. 80.

CORBISHLEY, S.J., T. ; 'What is Purity' ? Manresa Press, Roehampton. 6d.

GITS, S.J., A. ; 'Training for Marriage : A Book for Catholic Parents'. C.T.S., No. S.134.

HILDEBRAND, D. VON ; 'In Praise of Purity'.

KELLY, S.J., G. ; 'Chastity and Catholic Youth'. Bardgett Printing and Publishing Co., St. Louis, Mo. pp. 77.

LORD, S.J., Daniel A. ; 'Some Notes for the Guidance of Parents'. The Queen's Work, 3742 West Pine Boulevard, St. Louis 8, Mo. 1944. pp.252.

MAHONEY, D.D., Canon E. J. ; 'Training in Purity'. C.T.S., No. S.113.

McGOVERN, Cong. Orat., L. ; 'For Boys and Men'. C.T.S., No. Do.163.

MARTINDALE, S.J., C. C. ; 'The Difficult Commandment'. Manresa Press, Roehampton.

National Union of Teachers ; ' Sex Education in the Schools' (for over 16), Statement by the Executive of the National Union of Teachers. N.U.T., Hamilton House, Mabledon Place, W.C.1.

WALSH, M.D., Ph.D., J. H. ; 'Sex Instruction'. Herder, London, pp.219.

WINGFIELD HOPE, Mrs. ; 'Life Together'. Sheed & Ward, pp. 184.

Government Publications (Board of Education).

'The Youth Service after the War'. H.M.S.O. 1943, 6d.

'Sex Education in Schools and Youth Organisations'. H.M.S.O. 1943, 6d.

Central Council for Health Education Publications.

'The Approach to Womanhood'. Pp. 16. 3d. (For Girls over 16.)

'Manhood ; And Explanation of Sex for Young Men'. Pp. 20· 3d. (For over 16.)

'From Boyhood to Manhood'. Pp. 20. 3d. (For Boys under 16.)

'What shall I tell my child ?' Pp. 22.

'Yourself and your Body'. Pp. 16. 3d. (For Girls under 16.)

'Health Education in the School'. Pp. 24.

The above pamphlets may be obtained on application to the General Secretary, Central Council for Health Education, Tavistock House, Tavistock Square, London, W.C.1. Parents and teachers will find in them an accurate and adequate account of the necessary physiological facts. In suitable cases, and with due supplementary instruction, these pamphlets may be put into the hands of the young people themselves. In such cases, the pamphlet should be duly recovered by the adult concerned, since even the best and most reticent treatments of this subject are not suitable for indiscriminate circulation among irresponsible persons.

INDEX

INDEX

1. **A TWO YEAR PUBLIC MINISTRY.** Defended by Father EDMUND F. SUTCLIFFE, S.J., Professor of Holy Scripture at Heythrop College. 8s. 6d.

   Father Sutcliffe 'presents a scholarly view of the relevant evidence. . . . The book is a very useful contribution to an obscure subject'.—*The Congregational Quarterly.*

   'The author gives a detailed and scholarly treatment of a very difficult question. His work will be of great value to biblical students. The educated laity will also find it most interesting and instructive'.—*The Sign.*

   'The general construction of the work and the marshalling of the arguments should be a joy to all who have the privilege of studying it'.—*Irish News.*

   'Father Sutcliffe's book . . . is well worth reading, as it throws much light not only on this problem but on kindred questions of chronology.—*Buckfast Abbey Chronicle.*

2. **MORAL PROBLEMS OF MENTAL DEFECT.** By Father J. S. CAMMACK, S.J., Professor of Ethics at Heythrop College. 8s. 6d.

   'This valuable study of mental defect makes fascinating reading because of its logical precision and clarity of thought.'—*The Guardian.*

   'Father Cammack is to be thanked and congratulated for his masterly exposition of the problems at issue'.—*Blackfriars.*

   'This is a book to be recommended not only to moral theologians, but to all interested in the moral and social problems of mental defect and delinquency.'—*The Tablet.*

   'The work done is pioneer work, so far as the moral aspect of the problem goes. It is excellently done—balanced, scholarly and most readable'.—*The Irish Ecclesiastical Record.*

3. **THE ORACLES OF JACOB AND BALAAM.** By Father ERIC BURROWS, S.J., of Campion Hall, Oxford. 12s. 6d.

   'This book . . . is a masterpiece of Biblical exegesis. . . . The author's learning elicits . . . a flood of light on Old Testament history and prophecy'.—*The Tablet.*

   'This volume . . . bears testimony to his wide studies and keen intellect, and contains much that gives it more than ordinary interest'.—*The Journal of Theological Studies.*

   'The theory . . . has never been elaborated with such penetrating detail and insight as in the volume before us. . . It is particularly interesting to see how the meaning and significance of verse after verse becomes clear when the zodiacal allusion is explained'.—*The Guardian*.

4. ST. CYPRIAN'S *DE UNITATE*, CHAP. 4, IN THE LIGHT OF THE MANUSCRIPTS. By Father MAURICE BÉVENOT, S.J., Professor of Fundamental Theology at Heythrop College. 8s. 6d.

'The book is one to which all concerned with a fascinatingly difficult textual problem will turn with gratitude. . . . The tables and collections of data are invaluable'.—*The Times Literary Supplement*.

'The industry and research of the writer and his elaborate discussion of the manuscripts are worthy of the highest praise'. —*The Guardian*.

'This painstaking and detailed work . . . the most thorough examination of the manuscripts that has yet been made. . . . Every serious student of Cyprian must go to the book itself'.— A. Souter in *The Journal of Theological Studies*.

5. AN INTRODUCTION TO THE STUDY OF ASCETICAL AND MYSTICAL THEOLOGY. The Substance of Seventeen Lectures given at Heythrop College. By the Most Rev. ALBAN GOODIER, S.J., Archbishop of Hierapolis. 8s. 6d.

'The concluding section of Archbishop Goodier's book is certainly something which all who value mysticism would be the better for reading carefully. This description of infused prayer, identified here with the Unitive Way, does in fact say what in substance is traditional, yet in a completely fresh way'.—*The Tablet*.

'Archbishop Goodier's description of the inner life of the Christian is worth many a longer and more pretentious work, and may be heartily recommended to all who are seeking to make progress in the spiritual life or to help others to do so. It is the distilled wisdom of one who is master of his subject'.—*The Church Quarterly Review*.

6. THE GOSPEL OF THE INFANCY AND OTHER BIBLICAL ESSAYS. By Father ERIC BURROWS, S.J. 8s. 6d.

'This volume is "an important contribution to modern biblical studies. . . . These essays display Fr. Burrows' great learning and penetrating vision to the greatest advantage . . . (They) are as brilliant as they are painstaking and learned" '. —*The Downside Review*.

'The high standard of excellence attained in all the eight papers in the book . . . Fr. Burrows' accustomed brilliance'. —*The Tablet*.

7. **FRIEDRICH NIETZSCHE, PHILOSOPHER OF CULTURE.** By Father FREDERICK COPLESTON, S.J., Professor of the History of Philosophy at Heythrop College. 8s. 6d.

'Father Copleston's book on Nietzsche is one of the best expositions and discussions of that philosopher in the English language'.—Desmond MacCarthy in *The Sunday Times*.

'This book is an exposition . . . of unusual merit. . . . The author neither reads in what is not there nor glosses over the significance of what is there. . . . Can be recommended as an excellent introduction'.—Dr. J. Wisdom in *Mind*.

'This is a book many have, or should have been looking for· A study of Nietzsche from the Christian standpoint, scrupulously fair, and above all unbiassed by the too common desire to make anti-German capital out of Nietzsche by misrepresenting him as a Nazi before Hitler . . . such a study was badly needed, and here it is'.—*The Tablet*.

8. **THE OLD TESTAMENT AND THE FUTURE LIFE.** By Father EDMUND F. SUTCLIFFE, S.J., Professor of Scripture at Heythrop College. In the press.

9. **A HISTORY OF PHILOSOPHY. I. ANCIENT PHILOSOPHY.** By Father FREDERICK COPLESTON, S.J., Professor of the History of Philosophy at Heythrop College. In the press.

11. **ARTHUR SCHOPENHAUER, PHILOSOPHER OF PESSIMISM.** By Father FREDERICK COPLESTON, S.J.